Second Edition

BIOGRAPHY OF A TENEMENT HOUSE IN NEW YORK CITY

BIOGRAPHY OF A TENEMENT HOUSE

An Architectural History of 97 Orchard Street

Second Edition

by Andrew S. Dolkart

Center for American Places at Columbia College Chicago

The Center for American Places at Columbia College Chicago
600 South Michigan Avenue
Chicago, Illinois 60605-1996, U.S.A.

Distributed by the University of Virginia Press
www.upress.virginia.edu

20 19 18 17 16 15 14 13 12   1 2 3 4 5

ISBN: 978-1-935195-38-2

CONTENTS

To my immigrant grandparents David and Ida Luberg and Harry and Alice Dolkart

PREFACE AND ACKNOWLEDGMENTS

I trace my ancestry back to the Mayflower. Not to the legendary ship that brought the Pilgrims to Plymouth, Massachusetts, in 1620, but to the more prosaic tenement on the southeast corner of East Broadway and Clinton Street named the Mayflower, where my father was born in 1914 to Russian-Jewish immigrants. This Mayflower, with its name carved in the frieze of its entrance portico, was built in 1907—commissioned by a Jewish developer and designed by Jewish architects, with apartments rented to poor Jewish immigrants. Yet, somehow it is also a metaphor for the experience of immigrants and the children of immigrants from many backgrounds as they became part of the fabric of American life. Almost 100 years after its construction, the Mayflower and nearby Lower East Side tenements continue to house new immigrants, many from China, who face some of the same challenges as did their predecessors.

The Lower East Side Tenement Museum, housed in a tenement at 97 Orchard Street, celebrates the individuality of the immigrants who came to New York City in order to recreate their own lives and those of their families, and the universality of the immigrant experience from the mid-nineteenth century to today. The museum examines the lives of individual immigrants of the past—Irish, Germans, Jews, Italians, and others– each of whom contributed in a small way to New York City's diverse character, while also serving the educational needs of current immigrants who continue to invigorate the city.

I have been involved as an architectural historian with the Tenement

Museum since receiving a call from the museum's founder, Ruth J. Abram, in 1988. Abram asked if I would prepare a history of the tenement building at 97 Orchard Street that she hoped to transform into a museum. Thus began a complex project to document and interpret the physical history of a tenement built in the 1860s. Tenements were so common in New York City and their individual residents were traditionally seen as so inconsequential to the history of New York City and the United States that little attention had been paid to the specifics of the buildings' design, construction, and alteration. The building at 97 Orchard Street and its individual apartments were altered many times by owners and by residents, but little documentation recorded these changes. A history of the building would, therefore, have to rely on documentation that did exist, coupled with new research into housing reform and tenement laws, genealogical and archaeological research, and, most significantly, analysis of the physical fabric of the tenement itself. The apartments at 97 Orchard Street over time housed hundreds of families and thousands of individuals. The museum has chosen to interpret the lives of people who actually lived in the building. Thus, a history of the building must also incorporate a history of the families who made their lives there and contributed to the story of New York City and of the United States.

The success of this research project would have been impossible without the assistance of many people. Most significant is Ruth J. Abram, whose vision and commitment to establishing a house museum that would examine the lives of typical immigrants there made possible the Lower East Side Tenement Museum. Since 2008, her successor, Morris Vogel, has continued to bring visionary leadership to the institution. During the museum's formative years, Ruth Abram was ably assisted by curator Anita Jacobson, with whom I worked on an early history of the building. Several present and former members of the museum's staff have been especially important to first edition of this book and to this revised edition, always answering questions, editing manuscripts, and sharing their vast knowledge of 97 Orchard Street and immigrant issues in general. Most notable have been, Renee Epps, former executive vice president; David Favaloro, Director of Curatorial Affairs; Derya Golpinar, former archivist; Steve Long, former vice president for collections and education; Chris Neville, the coordinator of the investigation of the physical fabric of the basement; and Annie Polland, Vice President for Education. Archaeologist Joan Geismar generously responded to all of my queries about her discoveries during a backyard dig; paint conservators Janet Foster, Cynthia Hinson, and Mary Jablonski and wallpaper historian

Reba Fishman Snyder aided immeasurably in sorting out the history of room finishes in the building and analyzing what was original fabric and what had been added over time; and genealogist Marsha Dennis opened my ideas to a whole world of research into individual lives.

One of the great pleasures during the early years of the Tenement Museum project was the discussion of new ideas and interpretations with my friend and respected colleague, Judith Saltzman, of Li-Saltzman Architects, the museum's first architect and the firm responsible for all of the museum's initial stabilization and restoration projects. Besides Judith, I worked closely with her partner Roz Li, and with staff members, including Shika Jhaldiyal, Alex Wolfe, and John Favazzo.

It is always a joy undertaking research in New York City, where the resources are so bountiful. I would like to thank especially the activists at the Municipal Archives, notably Ken Cobb and Leonora Gidlund; the staff of Columbia University's Avery Architecture and Fine Arts Library; Ruth Carr and the reference librarians at the New York Public Library's American History, Local History and Genealogy Division and the librarians in the Map Division, especially the division's former chief librarian Alice Hudson; and the library staff at the New-York Historical Society. Early in the project, research assistance was provided by volunteers from the Junior League of New York.

Research for early versions of the history of 97 Orchard Street, including preparation of a history of the building for a Historic Structures Report, was partially funded by the National Endowment for the Humanities and by the J. M. Kaplan Fund. In addition, it is crucial to note the contribution of George F. Thompson, the founder of the Center for American Places at Columbia College Chicago, whose enthusiasm for the first edition of this book was unbounded, and Brandy Savarese who has shepherded the revised edition to completion.

Finally, I am especially indebted to the commitment of my husband Paris R. Baldacci, who has not only been supportive of my efforts to compete and then revise this publication, but improved every aspect of the text by his thoughtful and erudite editing of my work.

Andrew Dolkart
May 2012

Second Edition

BIOGRAPHY OF A TENEMENT HOUSE IN NEW YORK CITY

Figure 1. 97 Orchard Street, The Lower East Side Tenement Museum, 2005.
Courtesey of Lower East Side Tenement Museum (photograph by Keiko Niwa).

INTRODUCTION

The tenement house at 97 Orchard Street (Fig. 1), now the home of the Lower East Side Tenement Museum, is an extraordinary survivor from the first major wave of tenement construction in New York City in the 1860s and 1870s. In addition, this narrow building (less than twenty-five feet wide), with a simple brick facade rising only five stories plus a raised basement, is in the midst of a section of the Lower East Side that retains its historic context, having undergone little physical redevelopment since the early decades of the twentieth century. Surrounding blocks are densely packed with similar five- and six-story tenements that, over time, housed tens of thousands of immigrant households in their twenty or more small two- and three- room apartments. Although many tenements survive on the Lower East Side and in other New York City neighborhoods, the fact that 97 Orchard Street retains much of its historic fabric provides a unique opportunity to document, analyze, and interpret the housing conditions in which the urban poor lived from the mid-nineteenth century to the early decades of the twentieth century. Built in 1863, when residential construction was subject to only the most minimal regulation, 97 Orchard Street exemplifies the type of cramped and rudimentary multiple dwelling erected in enormous numbers to house tens of thousands of poor and working-class, mostly immigrant, households on the city's narrow lots.

In spite of the dire conditions at 97 Orchard Street, nearly 7,000 people lived and in some instances worked there from 1864 until 1935, when it ceased functioning as a residential building. Although most of these families did not remain in the tenement for long, 97 Orchard Street was their home, where they struggled to create an environment in which to raise their families. The personal and often economic success of so many of these immigrant families is a testament to their resilience in the face of the harsh realities of their daily lives.

While a few design and construction features of 97 Orchard Street were relatively up-to-date in 1864, other features were extremely dated. Even when new, it was poorly ventilated and contained minimal sanitary facilities. Beginning almost immediately after completion, changes were regularly made to the building's fabric. Some alterations merely reflected the need to maintain the building in order to maximize the owner's rental income; others were required by a series of housing reform laws enacted in the hope of improving living conditions for the residents of these structures. In either case, work was inevitably done in the least expensive way possible, often recycling older building elements. As the building aged and as the number of tenants increased, conditions deteriorated.

The evolution of tenement laws, the motives of the reformers who campaigned for their passage, and the general character of tenement designs and plans have been examined in great detail by many architectural and urban historians and by housing reformers themselves, most prominently by reformer Lawrence Veiller in his essay published in the influential 1903 *The Tenement House Problem in New York*; James Ford in his pioneering 1936 study *Slums and Housing*; Roy Lubove in *The Progressives and the Slums*; Anthony Jackson in *A Place Called Home*; and by Richard Plunz in his comprehensive *History of Housing in New York City*.[1] However, the specific impact that these laws had on individual buildings and the apartments in which people actually lived has not been explored in detail.[2] This short book attempts to fill that gap by critically examining the construction, alteration, and occupancy of 97 Orchard Street as a primary document for understanding the nature of tenement design and tenement life in New York City. The history of 97 Orchard Street is not identical to the histories of all tenements, since each privately owned tenement has its own history of design, construction, alteration, and residence. Nonetheless, many aspects of the history of 97 Orchard Street mirror the histories of other nineteenth-century tenements in New York City—so this singular building also tells a more universal story of tenement design and change, and of the lives of those who lived in these buildings.

EARLY DEVELOPMENT ON THE LOWER EAST SIDE

Manhattan's Lower East Side was not developed until the early decades of the nineteenth century. Before the Revolutionary War, the land on which 97 Orchard Street is located was part of the large farm belonging to the De Lancey family, which included much of the Lower East Side north of Division Street. By the late 1760s, the De Lanceys had established a street grid on a portion of their property, with the longer north-south streets generally paralleling the route of the nearby Bowery.[1] This grid established the street plan that would later be expanded north to Houston Street (Fig. 2). During the war, the De Lanceys had supported the British. Thus, after the war, in accordance with New York State's 1779 Act for the Forfeiture and Sale of the Estates of Persons who Have Adhered to the Enemies of this State, the farm was confiscated by New York City and then sold in several parcels between 1784 and 1786.[2] In the deeds of sale the city made no effort to restrict what could be built on these blockfronts. Thus, the former De Lancey Farm was developed with a mix of wooden buildings and brick row houses (Figs. 3–4). This mixture contrasted with development on the property to the south, the Rutgers Farm, which was separated from the former De Lancey property by Division Street, where the Rutgers family had laid out a separate grid (Fig. 2) and required more substantial brick row houses.[3]

Figure 2. A New & Accurate Plan of the City of New York [The Taylor-Roberts Map], 1796. The Lower East Side, at the right, is divided into two grids separated by Division Street. The future site of 97 Orchard Street is in the underdeveloped region east of Bowery Road. Courtesy of The Lionel Pincus and Princess Firyal Map Division, The New York Public Library, Astor Lenox and Tilden Foundations.

Some of the buyers of the former De Lancey properties quickly erected buildings, but others merely held the land, hoping to sell or lease it at a substantial profit as it became more valuable. The plot that would become 97 Orchard Street changed hands several times until it was acquired in December 1814, along with adjoining lots, by the renowned John Jacob Astor.[4] Astor, an immigrant from Waldorf, Germany, established one of the great New York fortunes, initially through fur trading. Beginning in 1810, Astor shrewdly invested in New York real estate, generally in undeveloped areas, from which he and his descendants reaped huge profits as new neighborhoods developed there.[5] In 1811, Astor purchased four twenty-five-foot-wide lots at what are now 95, 97, 99, and 101 Orchard Street between Broome and Delancey Streets. In 1828, Astor sold the three lots at 95–99 Orchard Street to the newly established Orchard Street Reformed Dutch Church.[6] The Reformed Dutch congregation erected a "very substantial" masonry church, described as "a very commodious house of worship," on a block

Figure 3. These early nineteenth-century wood and brick single-family homes on the Lower East Side had been converted into tenements by the time this photograph was taken in the early twentieth century. *Fourth Report of the Tenement House Department of New York* (1907). Courtesy of William Dailey.

Figure 4. "Old shanties," on the corner of Ludlow and Delancey Streets, one block from 97 Orchard Street, in 1864. D. T. Valentine, *Manual of the Corporation of the City of New York* (1864). Courtesy of Andrew S. Dolkart.

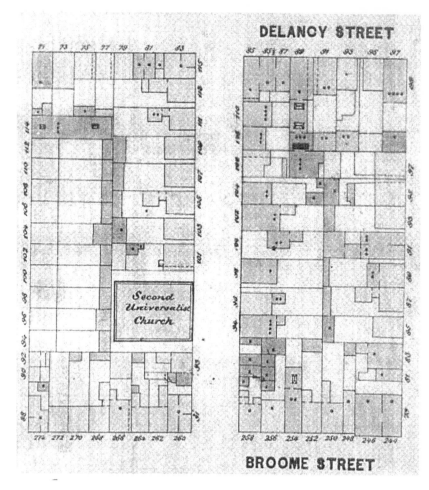

Figure 5. Map of Orchard Street between Delancey and Broome Streets, 1856, with the church at 95–99 Orchard Street surrounded primarily by wooden buildings. William Perris, Maps of the City of New York, vol. 1 (1856). Courtesy of Avery Architectural and Fine Arts Library, Columbia University in the City of New York.

that was otherwise filled almost entirely with small wooden houses (Fig. 5).[7] The new church, however, proved to be an unsuccessful venture by this Dutch Reformed congregation, which, burdened by debt, lost the property in a foreclosure action in 1831. In 1836, the property was transferred to the Second Universalist Society of New York, although this congregation occupied the building as early as 1832.[8] In 1860, having moved to East

11th Street, the Universalist congregation sold the building to the Second Reformed Presbyterian Church of New York. The decision by this Presbyterian congregation to buy the church building was short-sighted, since by the 1860s the religious composition of the Lower East Side's population was changing rapidly. With its increasing German immigrant community composed largely of Roman Catholics from Bavaria and other southern German states, Protestant adherents—mostly members of Lutheran and German Reformed congregations—from Prussia and other northern states, as well as a significant number of Jews, the neighborhood was no longer one where English-speaking Protestant denominations such as the Presbyterians were likely to attract many congregants.[9]

Much of the Protestant population that had settled on the Lower East Side earlier in the nineteenth century had moved north on Manhattan Island by the 1860s. Throughout the nineteenth century, the migration of New York City's affluent population north into developing neighborhoods had a significant impact both on the character of the newly popular areas and the older areas they had left. In the 1820s the Lower East Side was considered a fashionable residential neighborhood, but by the 1830s the area to the north around Bond Street and St. Mark's Place (in what is now the East Village) had become the city's most prestigious residential area. In the 1840s, prominent New Yorkers moved even farther north into the Gramercy Park area near East 23rd Street, while in the 1850s Murray Hill, located in the East 30s, was developed with substantial rowhouses.[10]

In the 1840s and 1850s, as more and more prosperous families were moving out of the Lower East Side, a major wave of immigrants was arriving in New York City. Between 1840 and 1850, New York City's population increased by more than sixty percent, from 312,710 to 515,547. By 1860, the population increased an additional 57.8 percent, rising to 813,669.[11] A substantial proportion of the new arrivals were Irish and German immigrants, many of whom settled on the Lower East Side, where the exodus of residents had resulted in the widespread availability of housing. The Tenth Ward, the area north of Division Street and east of the Bowery that includes the block on which 97 Orchard Street is located, soon became the center of the new immigrant German community. Since most immigrants could not afford to rent an entire single-family house, the row houses were either converted into multiple dwellings or replaced by new multi-family dwellings referred to as "tenements."

Among the first generation of tenements built in the Tenth Ward were three buildings erected in 1863 on the site of the Orchard Street church.

On February 28, 1863, the Second Reformed Presbyterian Church sold its building to three developers, all of whom were tailors who had immigrated from Germany: Lucas Glockner, Adam Stumm, and Jacob Walter. Glockner, Stumm, and Walter purchased the church property as joint owners, but then immediately divided it into three separately owned units, each 24'-10 1/3" wide by 88' 6" deep, corresponding to the three lots that the Dutch Reformed Church had combined in 1828. Jacob Walter received no. 95; Lucas Glockner no. 97, and Adam Stumm no. 99.[12] The church building was soon demolished. All three men immediately erected tenements on their lots. Walter built an individual five-story tenement, while Glockner and Stumm erected a pair of identical five-story raised basement buildings (Fig. 6). The 1864 tax assessments record that Glockner and Stumm's properties were each valued at $8,000, while Walter's somewhat smaller building was worth $1,000 less.[13] Construction must have taken place quite rapidly, for by late 1863, 97 Orchard Street was already occupied. Sadly, the first reference to the building and its inhabitants in city records is a death certificate for six-month-old Eliza Berkley, dated October 20, 1863.[14]

Figure 6. 95–99 Orchard Street, 1939. Courtesy of New York City Municipal Archives.

THE TENEMENT AND ITS INHABITANTS

"Tenement" is both a legal term codified in city regulations, and a word commonly used to refer to a certain type of multi-family housing. The first official definition of tenement—or, as it was commonly termed in the nineteenth and early twentieth centuries, "tenement house"—in New York City is found in the Tenement House Law of 1867: "Every house, building, or portion thereof which is rented, leased, let or hired out to be occupied or is occupied as the home or residence of more than three families living independently of another, and doing their cooking upon the premises, or by more than two families upon a floor, so living and cooking, but having a common right in the halls, stairways, yards, water-closets or privies, or some of them."[1] In 1887, this definition was officially expanded to include also those buildings that housed just three families.[2] This broad definition can apply to almost all of New York City's multiple dwellings, even those such as the late nineteenth-century Dakota on Central Park West and West 72nd Street, and the Osborne on West 57th Street and Seventh Avenue, or the luxury apartment houses on Fifth and Park Avenues erected in the second and third decades of the twentieth century—all of which had expansive, well-appointed apartments. Such multiple dwellings, designed for the city's upper middle class and wealthiest households, were referred to in common parlance first as "flats" or "French flats," and later simply as "apartment houses."[3] The term "tenement" generally refers only to those multiple dwellings built for the poor and which contained few, if any, of the amenities demanded by wealthier apartment dwellers such as private toilets, running water, gas lines, and one or more windows in every room. In his December 31, 1862 report, the Superintendent of Buildings provided one of the most succinct definitions of a tenement: a building where "the greatest amount of profit is sought to be realized from the least possible amount of space, with little or no regard for the health, comfort, or protection of the lives of the tenants."[4]

Many factors contributed to the substandard living conditions in New York City's overcrowded tenement neighborhoods. The root of the problem, however, lay both in the division of New York City's blocks into narrow building lots and in the pattern of individual lot ownership that resulted from this division. During the seventeenth and much of the eighteenth centuries, New York City had been a relatively small colonial settlement located at the southern tip of Manhattan Island, with buildings erected along a haphazard street pattern. As the city's population grew and residential neighborhoods were established to the north of the old settlement, landowners laid out streets on a series of varied grid plans (see Fig. 2).[5] Each block was divided into individual lots that were typically twenty-five feet wide by up to one hundred feet deep. These lots were then sold or leased to owners or developers, who generally erected single-family row houses. Often they would build one row house on each lot, although they also frequently acquired several lots and squeezed a larger number of narrower single-family homes on the combined lots.

The 25' by 100' lot size was fairly generous for an individual single-family row house. Only later, with the construction of tenements built to house twenty or more households, was this small building lot considered by some to be a problem. By the late nineteenth century, the noted architect Ernest Flagg, one of the leaders of the tenement reform movement, wrote: "The greatest evil which ever befell New York City was the division of the blocks into 25 x 100 feet. So true is this, that no other disaster can for a moment be compared with it. Fires, pestilence and financial troubles are nothing in comparison, for from this division has arisen the New York system of tenement-houses, the worst curse which ever afflicted any great community."[6] The exact date of construction of the first purpose-built tenement in Manhattan is unknown, but it is often traced as far back to the 1820s or 1830s.[7] By the 1840s, the number of tenements, including both older converted single-family homes and new purpose-built structures, had increased significantly.[8] The resulting crowded and deteriorated living conditions in tenement areas such as the notorious Five Points became so severe that residents of New York City's more affluent neighborhoods became increasingly concerned about their impact on the rest of the city. In 1842, Dr. John H. Griscom, the City Inspector of the Board of Health, was the first to investigate and publicly discuss conditions in tenement districts.[9] The following year, the Association for Improving the Condition of the Poor (AICP), the first charitable organization to focus the attention of the city's affluent residents on conditions in tenement districts, was established. As tenement reformer Lawrence Veiller noted in 1903, in reference to the founding of the AICP, "prior to this time [1843], the dwellings of the poor had not been a subject of interest or attention on the part of the more fortunate members of the community, little attention being paid to their condition except by the City Inspector and by those members of the clergy whose labors took them among the poor as 'City Missionaries.'"[10] In his history of tenement reform, Veiller quotes from an early AICP report containing one of the first discussions of the conditions in which tenement dwellers lived: the "tenements of the poor in this city are generally defective in size, arrangement, supplies of water, warmth, and ventilation; also the yards, sinks [i.e., outdoor toilets], and sewage are in bad condition."[11] What is especially noteworthy about this description is that although written in the 1840s, it accurately describes tenement conditions in 1900. In fact, many descriptions of the Lower East Side in the late nineteenth and early twentieth centuries document the same problems: overcrowding, a lack of light, air, and water, and inadequate toilets and sewerage.

During the 1850s and 1860s, few efforts were made to improve conditions in tenement house districts. In 1855, the AICP erected the first "model tenement," the Workingmen's Home, a six-story building located on a narrow through-block site from Mott Street to Elizabeth Street, north of Canal Street, which initially housed African-American families.[12] Although this particular model tenement was sold in the late 1860s and soon deteriorated, it established a precedent for privately built model housing. This approach was developed later in the nineteenth century and into the early twentieth century by Alfred T. White at his Home, Tower, and Riverside projects near the Brooklyn waterfront; by Charles Pratt at his Astral Apartments in Greenpoint, Brooklyn; and by the City and Suburban Homes Company, the Improved Dwellings Association, the Open Stair Dwellings Company, and other organizations.[13]

Although these experimental projects were often successful in providing decent housing, only a limited number were erected because the quality of their design and construction, and the provision of amenities, proved to be too costly for the developers. In addition, since the mission of the privately funded model tenement companies focused on creating decent housing rather than on building housing that would maximize profit, they limited the return on investment to between five and seven percent. As such, the model tenements could never be as profitable as speculative tenements. Thus it was speculative buildings, with their potential for profits of ten percent and more, that constituted the bulk of low-rent housing in the late nineteenth and early twentieth centuries.[14]

In 1862, in response to the city's deplorable housing conditions, the New York State Legislature established the New York City Department of Buildings and mandated, for the first time, minimum standards for building construction. All buildings erected after May 1, 1862, including tenements, were supposed to adhere to such basic requirements as party walls of stone, brick, or iron; use of quality mortar; minimum thickness for walls; minimum size for structural members; adequate fire escapes; and standards for doors, windows, and cornices.[15] Two years after the formation of the Department of Buildings, a group of leading New Yorkers organized the Citizens' Association "for the purpose of taking steps to improve the sanitary condition of the city."[16] The association formed a subcommittee known as the Council of Hygiene and Public Health, which in 1864 conducted the first survey of housing and sanitary conditions in New York City. In order to complete this survey, the council divided the city into sanitary inspection districts and sent a sanitary inspector to examine conditions in each area. The survey, analyzing conditions in each sanitary district, took nine months to complete.[17] A comprehensive report was issued in January 1865; the report proved to be so popular that a second edition was published in 1866. The report described just how appalling conditions were in some of the city's most crowded wards.[18] Since the Council of Hygiene and Public Health's survey was begun in the same year that 97 Orchard Street was completed, it documents housing conditions in New York City at the same time this building was erected and first inhabited.

The Council found that as of December 1864, when its survey was completed, 495,592 people in New York City, out of a total population of 813,669, lived in what it referred to as "tenant-houses."[19] It further documented that there were 15,309 tenant-houses in the city with an average of 7 1/6 families in each.[20] In regard to the residential population density, the report stated:

> The tenant-house population is actually packed upon the house-lots and streets at the rate of 240,000 to the square mile; and it is only because this rate of

packing is somewhat diminished by intervening warehouses, factories, private dwellings, and other classes of buildings; that the entire tenement-house population is not devastated by the domestic pestilences and infectious epidemics that arise from overcrowding and uncleanness. . . . Such concentration and packing of a population has probably never been equalled in any city as may be found in particular localities in New York.[21]

The report also compared New York City's statistics with those prepared by the Royal Commission for London. East London, the most densely populated area of that city, was found to have a density of 175,816 people per square mile. That number is substantially lower than that of New York City's most densely populated wards, including the Tenth Ward, the area bound by Rivington Street on the north, Division Street on the south, Norfolk Street on the east, and the Bowery on the west, where 97 Orchard Street is located. In 1864, the density of the Tenth Ward was 240,000 people per square mile.[22] This figure, it should be noted, reflects the population density of the Tenth Ward prior to major new tenement construction in the ensuing decades that would substantially increase its population.

Dr. J. T. Kennedy was the inspector for the Eighth Sanitary Inspection District, an area coterminous with the Tenth Ward. The results of his report provide graphic evidence of living conditions in this increasingly crowded neighborhood. The survey documented 534 tenements in the Tenth Ward with a total tenement population of 18,140.[23] Although only one-fifth of the buildings in the ward were tenements, the large new tenements and the older houses that had been converted into tenements had the city's highest average number of families per tenement.

Kennedy found that the population of the ward was primarily German.[24] Indeed, there were so many German speakers living in the Tenth Ward that it became known as *Kleindeutschland* (Little Germany). As the survey states:

> This part of our city at one time was inhabited by some of our most respected citizens of moderate ideas, confined to houses of two stories in height; but time has changed the whole character of the inhabitants. The "Teutonic" race seems to have rushed in here in sufficient numbers to predominate, and landholders have found it profitable to erect very many substantial tenant-houses, to accommodate the increase of the population. . . . [Visitors] will be astonished at the immensity of the vast throngs of orderly, and cleanly, well-dressed people, and be struck with the excellent sanitary condition, as evinced by the[ir] healthful appearance.[25]

Early information regarding the residents of 97 Orchard Street confirms the dominance of German speakers in the area. The first records that provide evidence of the population that moved into the newly completed building are Civil War draft registers from 1864. These incomplete records document eight residents of 97 Orchard Street, six from Germany and two from Ireland.[26] This registry was followed in 1870 by the United States census enumeration of 97 Orchard Street, the first comprehensive official record of the tenement's residents. The census documents occupancy by seventy-two individuals in twenty households ranging in size from one to seven people. Most of those identified by the census enumerator were immigrants or the young children of immigrants from German-speaking states (prior to German unification in 1871, German speakers lived in a variety of large and small independent principalities). The largest number of German immigrants living at 97 Orchard Street came from Prussia, with smaller numbers from Baden and Wurttemberg and one resident from Bavaria. There were also several immigrants who had been born in Russia, probably in German-speaking regions.[27] Some of the men listed as heads of household were artisans, employed in skilled trades such as jeweler, boot and shoe maker, and surgical instrument maker. These were among the "mechanics" whom Inspector Kennedy found "predominate in this district."[28] These men probably earned a decent wage, but not enough to pay the rent on a single-family home. Other early residents of 97 Orchard Street made their livings through less skilled jobs—four, for example, were listed as peddlers. While most of the married women were described as "keeping house," a few young women were employed in sewing-related fields, including tassel-making and millinery.[29]

Among the German immigrants recorded in the 1870 census were Julius and Nathalie Gumpertz. Julius Gumpertz arrived in New York from East Prussia in 1857 or 1858 and soon after married Nathalie Rheinberg (Fig. 7), another Prussian immigrant who had arrived in the city at about the same time. Julius had trained as a shoemaker in Prussia, but as mechanization replaced the hand manufacturing of shoes, Julius left this business and opened a small store. By 1870, Julius and Nathalie had moved into a third-floor apartment at 97 Orchard Street with their two young children; two more children were born there over the next few years. The economic depression of 1873 had a serious impact on the Gumpertz family, forcing Julius to close his store and take a job as a heel cutter in a shoe factory. On October 7, 1874, Julius left for work at 7:00 am and never returned to the family. Although Julius's whereabouts were unknown to Nathalie, his name appears in an 1890 city directory for Cincinnati, where his occupation is listed as "huckster," a popular term for a peddler. By 1900, Julius had moved into the Jewish Home for the Aged & Infirm in Cincinnati, where he died in 1924 at the age of eighty-seven. Even in death, Julius hid the fact that he was married and had a family; his death certificate states that he was single.[30]

Figure 7: Nathalie Gumpertz, ca. 1890, after she had moved out of 97 Orchard Street. Courtesy of Lower East Side Tenement Museum.

Abandoned by the family's breadwinner, Nathalie opened a dressmaking business in her tenement apartment. In 1883, Julius's father died in Germany, leaving a bequest of $600 to his son. In order to inherit the money, Nathalie went to court requesting that her husband be declared legally dead. Among those who testified in support of her application were Lucas Glockner, owner of 97 Orchard Street, and John Schneider, who ran a saloon in the basement of the tenement. Soon after she won her case, Nathalie and her family left 97 Orchard Street and moved to Yorkville, the neighborhood in the East 70s and 80s, east of Third Avenue, where new tenements were being built that attracted a substantial German population.[31]

John Schneider, who testified on behalf of Nathalie Gumpertz, ran a saloon at 97 Orchard Street from 1864 until 1886. The presence of Schnieder's saloon in the commercial basement of the building substantiates Inspector Kennedy's remark that the Germans "brought with them from the 'Fatherland' all of their institutions, not excepting *lager bier.*"[32] Indeed, Kennedy counted 526 drinking establishments in the Tenth Ward and in 1872, the police department counted 726 in the area.[33] One writer, discussing German New York in 1862, described how when walking along the primarily German streets of the Lower East Side, one would pass brightly lit locals [neighborhood saloons] which are very lively. Through the shop window you see the German worker sitting around a large table with his whole family – and ranting about politics. The little boy, who is just tall enough to reach the table edge, has a mighty tankard of "lager" . . . in front of him and the Herr Papa views his youngest with satisfaction while the Frau Mama stuffs his mouth with pretzels and refreshes herself with a cool drink.[34]

Schneider took over the saloon at 97 Orchard Street from German Henry Schurlein, who had operated the establishment for only a single year. On November 11, 1864, Schneider placed an advertising notice in the *New Yorker Staats-Zeitung*, the city's leading German-language daily newspaper, announcing "to his fine friends and acquaintances as well as the honorable musicians, that he has taken over by purchase the saloon of Mr. Schurlein, 97 Orchard Street. Invited to the opening, Saturday, November 12th with a superb lunch."[35] The invitation to musicians is notable, both because Schneider was himself a musician, having served in the regimental band of the largely German-born 8th New York Infantry Volunteers in 1861–62, during the Civil War, but also because music played a key role in most German saloons. Brass bands, small musical ensembles, and singing societies often performed and customers frequently sang along with the musicians.[36] Schneider's saloon, like others in the neighborhood, also served as a social and political gathering place and meeting venue for some of the many clubs, or *vereins*, that flourished in German communities. In 1870, a notice in the *Staats-Zeitung* informed readers of a forthcoming meeting at 97 Orchard Street of the United Order of Red Men, the German American wing of a native patriotic organization. Three years later, in 1873, the *Staats-Zeitung* published information about a meeting in Schneider's saloon where officers and delegates were elected to the *Deutsch-Amerikanischer Reformverein*, an anti-Tammany political reform group.[37]

Schneider's saloon occupied the entire front of the basement; only in later years was the space divided into two stores. This was confirmed by research undertaken in 2010. A pair of cast-iron structural columns support a wooden beam that runs down the center of the basement space from front to back. The earliest four layers of paint on these columns are continuous around their entire circumference, indicating that they were originally freestanding.[38] The space probably had an oak or mahogany bar along one wall. Wooden tables and chairs would have been arrayed around the space for the comfort and sociability of families who frequented these important ethnic social centers. The cast-iron columns, chair rails (surviving on the south wall), beams, and other features of the interior were grained to give the appearance of expensive woodwork, a treatment similar to that applied to the woodwork in the apartments on the building's upper floors. The plaster walls were painted with a light grayish olive-colored base coat topped with a yellowish brown translucent glaze; near the ceiling was a decorative dark red and blue border.[39] Schneider not only ran the saloon, but he, his Prussian-born wife Caroline, and their son Harry, born in 1877, also lived at 97 Orchard Street, probably in one of the two basement apartments located to the rear of the saloon.[40] John Schneider would have managed the bar, while Caroline Schneider would have been responsible for the food offered to bring customers into the saloon and entice them into ordering multiple drinks, The food was undoubtedly prepared in the family's kitchen, located in the rear apartment. German residents of 97 Orchard Street frequented this conveniently located saloon. Schneider was clearly well acquainted with Nathalie Gumpertz. Real estate broker Heinrich Dreyer who lived upstairs is recorded at a meeting of the *Deutsch-Amerikanischer Reformverein* in Schneider's establishment, where he was elected a delegate.

Not every resident of 97 Orchard Street was German. A few Irish immigrants also lived here, although the heart of the Irish Lower East Side was several blocks to the south and to the west.[41] The 1864 Civil War draft records, previously sited, indicate two Irish immigrants in the building. The 1870 census lists one Irish immigrant, Mary Shepard, the wife of English laborer John Shepard.[42] One year earlier, however, a New York City directory listed 97 Orchard Street as the home of Joseph Peter Moore. The twenty-year-old Moore had come to New York in 1865 and shortly after met and married Bridget Meehan, who had arrived in New York two years earlier at the age of seventeen. Joseph worked as a waiter and bartender, but never made much money. When the Moores moved into 97 Orchard Street they had three daughters, including Agnes, who had been born only a few months before and had been baptized at St. Patrick's Cathedral on Mott Street. Tragically, Agnes died in the Orchard Street apartment, one of several Moore children who succumbed to diseases associated with malnutrition. Her death certificate gives the cause of death as marasmus, possibly caused by dehydration resulting from drinking contaminated milk. The Moores did not live at 97 Orchard Street for very long. Almost every year the family moved to a different building on the Lower East Side—perhaps, as with many other poor New Yorkers, to avoid paying a month's rent.[43]

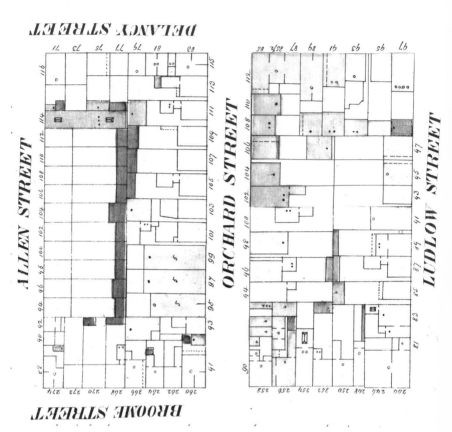

Figure 8. Map of Orchard Street between Delancey and Broome Streets, ca. 1863, after the church at 95–99 Orchard Street had been replaced by three large tenements. William Perris, *Maps of the City of New York,* vol. 1 (1859, updated to ca. 1863). Courtesy of The Lionel Pincus and Princess Firyal Map Division, The New York Public Library, Astor Lenox and Tilden Foundations.

3

DESIGN AND CONSTRUCTION
OF 97 ORCHARD STREET

Just as J. T. Kennedy was undertaking his survey of housing conditions in the Tenth Ward in 1864, the area was experiencing the beginning of a major boom in tenement construction. Among these new tenements were the three, five-story buildings erected by Glockner, Stumm, and Walter at 95–99 Orchard Street. Prior to the construction of such five-story tenements in the 1860s, most tenements were either converted row houses or new three- or four-story structures. Thus the three Orchard Street buildings were part of the first wave of large tenements, each housing approximately twenty families, to be erected in New York City.

In 1863, the size of the block bounded by Orchard, Allen, Broome, and Delancey Streets on which Glockner, Stumm, and Walter built their tenements was considerably larger than the narrow 253' by 88' rectangle that now exists, measuring approximately 353' by 175', with the longer frontages on Orchard and Allen Streets. In the nineteenth century, all four boundary streets were typical Lower East Side thoroughfares, measuring fifty-four feet from lot line to lot line (Delancey and Allen Streets are now wide boulevards).[1] Nos. 95–99 Orchard Street were near the southern end of the block, with eight building lots to the north.[2] The three tenements at 95–99 Orchard are the oldest extant buildings on this block and were the first new tenements built along the Orchard Street frontage (Fig. 8).[3]

These tenements were erected during the Civil War, at a time when new construction was declining in New York City. In the twelve months prior to the organization of the Department of Buildings on May 1, 1862, it is estimated that 2,250 buildings were erected in Manhattan. In 1863 the number had declined to 1,247, while in the following year construction began on only 755 buildings.[4] Nos. 95–99 Orchard Street were three of fifty-five tenements begun in the Tenth Ward in 1863; in the following year, only nine tenements were erected.[5] The largest number of tenements in the Tenth Ward were constructed in the years just after the Civil War, culminating in the years prior to the onset of national financial panic and depression in 1873.

The families in the new tenements lived in apartments with minimal space, light, and air, few amenities, and crowding. The conditions in such buildings were, however, often an improvement over conditions in converted row houses, which had not been designed for multiple tenancies and which, by the 1860s, were aged and deteriorated. James D. McCabe, Jr., in his 1872 description of various aspects of life in New York City, noted this contrast between the two classes of tenements—the new buildings, which were "immense, but spruce looking structures," and the converted houses, which were "simply dens of vice and misery." But McCabe reported that even the better class of tenements suffered "from the evils incident to and inseparable from such close packing, especially the impossibility of keeping a building with so many residents clean."[6] Conditions in the new tenement houses were also generally better than those available to the poor, especially the rural poor in the European states from which most Lower East Side immigrants hailed. In Europe, these immigrants had frequently lived in shacks with no sanitary facilities at all. The relative attractiveness of the apartments at 97 Orchard Street may explain why Lucas Glockner, the builder of this tenement, moved with his wife and young son from a converted row house at 119 St. Marks Place into the building at its completion. The Glockners remained there for a few years before moving into another tenement that Lucas owned at 25 Allen Street. An older son from a previous marriage, Edward Glockner, a bookbinder, and his Saxon-born wife, Caroline, remained in an apartment at 97 Orchard Street.

Lucas Glockner, a working-class German Lutheran immigrant with a small amount of capital, was probably typical of the hundreds of investors active in the construction of Lower East Side tenements.[7] Much tenement construction, ownership, and management in the nineteenth century and in the early decades of the twentieth century was undertaken by small entrepreneurs who were members of the same ethnic groups as those who rented apartments in the buildings. Thus, much of the construction on the Lower East Side in the 1860s and 1870s was undertaken by German and Irish builders for German and Irish owners, and the early residents were also primarily German and Irish. Glockner's real estate investments—which, besides 97 Orchard Street, included at least four other Lower East Side tenements (23–29 Allen Street, now demolished)—proved to be quite successful. The 1870 census records his personal wealth at $1,800, far higher than other families living at no. 97. In addition, his real estate holdings were valued at $45,000.[8] He retained ownership of 97 Orchard Street for twenty-three years, selling it in 1886 for $29,000.[9] Glockner's long-term retention of the tenement was unusual, since most tenement builders sought quick profit, selling the buildings shortly after they were completed and leaving it to others to profit over the long term from rental income. For example, Adam Stumm, Glockner's partner who erected the identical tenement at 99 Orchard Street, sold his building in 1867.

If an architect was associated with the design and construction of 97 Orchard Street, his name remains unknown.[10] Building permits for similar five-story tenements erected immediately after such recording was instituted in mid-1865, however, indicate that an architect was always involved with tenement construction. These architects were generally obscure practitioners, most of whom were immigrants, many from Germany. Some of these men (all architects identified as having worked on tenements were men) may have been trained as builders; others may have studied architecture in Europe before moving to the United States, where they chose to design for their fellow immigrants or could only find work designing these tenements.[11] These architects did not design buildings in the creative sense that we think of the practice of architecture today. The architects involved with tenements did not design the facades or the interior finishes. Rather, they probably chose the finishes and details, purchasing window lintels and sills, cornices, iron railings, cast-iron columns, wood wainscot, and other details at building yards or from manufacturers and foundries. Indeed, it is not uncommon to find identical tenement facades that are associated with the names of different architects.

Glockner's tenement at 97 Orchard Street and Stumm's identical building to the north extend back sixty-eight feet on the original 88'-6" deep lots. Their facades were designed in an extremely simplified version of the Italianate style, which was the most common style of architecture for buildings erected in New York City during the early 1860s.[12] By the time the tenement at 97 Orchard Street was built, Italianate-style features—

such as a general horizontal massing of facade elements and a use of arched openings, projecting stone lintels, and deeply projecting cornice with foliate brackets—had begun to be used even on the most modest building projects. Unlike the Italianate brownstone row houses erected in large numbers during the 1850s and 1860s for affluent households, however, and the marble and cast-iron commercial palazzi erected in the burgeoning commercial districts now known as Tribeca and SoHo, tenements were almost always faced with less expensive brick. Stone trim was used sparingly, if at all.

No. 97 Orchard Street is a five-story brick building set on a raised basement (see Fig. 1). The basement originally consisted of two wood storefronts, each flanked by cast-iron piers.[13] Wide stairs led down from the street to display windows and the shop doors. Above the basement, the street facade was constructed of red face-brick with lime-rich white mortar. The building originally had a

Figure 9. 97 Orchard Street, detail of front elevation, showing facade windows with original projecting lintels and sills, 1939. Courtesy of New York City Municipal Archives.

centrally placed first-floor entrance reached by a steep stone stoop. The entry was framed by a segmental-arch stone surround with modest projecting moldings. Flanking the entrance were single segmental-arch windows. The entrance, flanking windows, and stoop were all replaced in 1905 when shop fronts were added to the first story; similar changes were made to other tenements with raised first floors as owners sought to increase the percentage of their income from commercial rentals. The largely intact upper facade is four bays wide with horizontal bands of segmental-arch windows (Fig. 9), each with a modest projecting brownstone lintel and sill (all were shaved back, undoubtedly as a result of deterioration to the soft sandstone). Each window had a double-hung, two-over-two wood sash originally painted

Figure 10. 97 Orchard Street, Italianate-style cornice originally painted in imitation of brownstone, ca. 2000. Courtesy of Lower East Side Tenement Museum.

creamy white with a finish coat of varnish.[14] The street facade was crowned by a projecting metal cornice (Fig. 10) coated with a brownstone-colored paint onto which sand, comprised of small clear quartz particles, was blown while the paint was still wet, thus assuring that the inexpensive metalwork resembled stone.[15] Although the cornice was designed with Italianate acanthus-leaf brackets, modillions, and rosettes, their presence does not reflect an effort on the part of the tenement builder to create a fashionable, architecturally distinguished structure. Rather, cornices with this design were stock items in the 1860s, widely available from builders' yards.

The rear elevation was even simpler than the front. The rear wall, built of common brick laid with a coarse mortar, was articulated by rectangular window openings with simple flat lintels and slightly projecting sills. The rear window frames were also painted creamy white. In the center of the first floor was a doorway from which wooden stairs originally led to the rear yard. An additional rear door connected the commercial establishments in the basement with the yard. The yard, which was paved with stone blocks, was the location of the building's privies and had a water hydrant.[16] It was also the place where women gathered and socialized while doing their laundry (Fig. 11). The tenement's cellar was connected to the yard by a stone stair.

As required by the 1862 law, an iron fire escape was originally attached to the front elevation (Fig. 12). The fire escape at 97 Orchard Street was an

Figure 11. Backyard of a group of tenements on Elizabeth Street with school sinks at right, ca. 1903. William De Forest and Lawrence Veiller, eds., *The Tenement House Problem* (1903). Courtesy of Andrew S. Dolkart.

early example of fire escape design, known as a fire ladder. Instead of the stairs found on most fire escapes, that at 97 Orchard Street employed vertical ladders connecting each floor. Reformers considered these fire ladders to be unsafe, since children and older people would have trouble using them. Veiller and reformer Hugh Bonner suggested that "in no case should vertical ladders be permitted."[17] New fire ladders were finally banned in 1901, but those in place were permitted to remain.[18] Another fire ladder was located outside of a window of each of the rear apartments on the south side of 97

Orchard Street. The adjoining north apartment in the rear has a "party-wall balcony" that links 97 and 99 Orchard Street (Fig. 13). In case of a fire in no. 97, the residents of the north apartments were supposed to climb onto the balconies and escape by entering the apartments in number 99.[19] Such party-wall balconies were once common on tenements erected in groups with all floors aligned; many can still be seen on the Lower East Side and in other tenement neighborhoods of New York City.

Fire protection and the installation of fire escapes was a major concern of reformers in the second half of the nineteenth century and first decades of the twentieth century, since fire was, as the *New York Times* noted, an "ever-present tenement horror."[20] In the year beginning November 1, 1899, forty-one people died in tenement fires and large numbers of families were displaced.[21] Bonner, Veiller, and other reformers advocated for fireproof construction in all tenements and also for fire escapes that would be entirely built of fireproof metal (many early fire escapes had wooden balcony floors), and would have easily accessible stairs leading from apartment windows to the ground. The adequacy of the fire escapes and balconies was,

Figure 12. 97 Orchard Street, detail of frontispiece, showing fire escape in the form of a ladder, 1939. The fire escape was removed in about 1980. Courtesy of New York City Municipal Archives.

however, not the only problem with these structures. Equally problematic was the fact that fire escapes were often encumbered with boxes,

Figure 13. Party-wall balcony connecting rear windows of 97 (right) and 99 Orchard Street, 2005. Photograph by Andrew S. Dolkart.

barrels, and household utensils (Fig. 14), and were frequently used for airing or storing bedding (Fig. 15). Other large items, such as washbasins, were also frequently stored outside, often hung from hooks nailed into the brick or mortar (Fig. 16), some of which also blocked the fire escapes. While storing items on fire escapes and tenement walls was illegal, the laws were widely ignored, especially by tenants who lived in rear units where their possessions would not be seen from the street. According to the Fire Department, "the work of the firemen in rescuing tenants is often impeded by such encumbrances."[22] However, tenants in small tenement apartments generally ignored the danger of fire, treating the fire escapes and rear walls as extensions of their apartments, undoubtedly welcoming the additional storage space.

In addition to fire escapes, the 1862 law mandated another possible means of escaping a fire, requiring a narrow door inside each tenement apartment connecting the front and rear units (Fig. 17). In case of a fire, residents in one apartment were supposed to escape through the neighboring unit. At 97 Orchard Street these doors are located in small inner bedrooms and are extant on the north side of the structure. The practicality of

Figure 14. Fire escapes encumbered with boxes, barrels, and other objects. William De Forest and Lawrence Veiller, eds., *The Tenement House Problem* (1903). Courtesy of Andrew S. Dolkart.

these doors as escape routes must have been negligible, since owners fashioned informal locks and the tiny bedrooms contained so much furniture and bedding that it would have been exceedingly difficult to open the door in case of emergency.

Like the exterior design, the interior plan of the tenement at 97 Or-

Figure 15. Tenement residents frequently aired their bedding on the fire escapes, as is evident on the fire balconies of the tenements on Orchard Street just north of Rivington Street, ca. 1905. Courtesy of The Irma and Paul Milstein Division of United States, Local History and Genealogy (Tenement House Commission Collection), The New York Public Library, Astor Lenox and Tilden Foundations.

Figure 16. Washbasins are hung from hooks on the rear facades of a group of Lower East Side tenements; fire escapes are encumbered by household equipment, including a metal coffee pot (center). The windows overlook a lot used for the storage of pushcarts, ca. 1905. Courtesy of The Irma and Paul Milstein Division of United States, Local History and Genealogy (Tenement House Commission Collection), The New York Public Library, Astor Lenox and Tilden Foundations.

Figure 17. 97 Orchard Street, fire door connecting the inner bedrooms of two separate tenement apartments, ca. 2000. Courtesy of Lower East Side Tenement Museum.

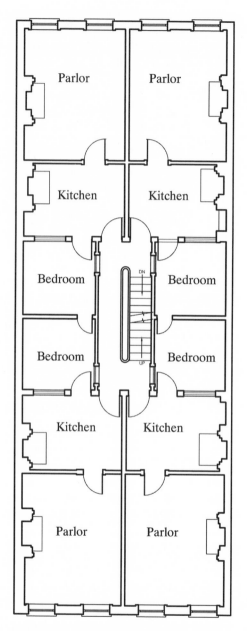

Figure 18. Plan of the four apartments on the upper four floors of 97 Orchard Street at the time of the building's completion in 1863. Courtesy of Li-Saltzman Architects.

Figure 19. Entrance hall at 97 Orchard Street in 2005, with original wood wainscot, plaster arch supported on brackets, and stair rail. The wall covering and floor tiles probably date from 1905. Photograph by Andrew S. Dolkart.

chard Street typifies those erected on the Lower East Side in the 1860s and 1870s (Fig. 18).[23] The building contained twenty apartments on five residential floors; each floor contained four apartments, two in the front and two in the rear. In addition, there were two apartments behind the commercial space in the basement. The apartments were extremely small. On

the second through fifth floors, the kitchens and living rooms were approximately twelve feet wide, with each apartment totaling only about 350 square feet. Apartments in the basement and on the first floor were even smaller, since public halls ran through the building on these levels, leaving a width of only about nine to ten feet for the front apartments and ten feet for the rear apartments where the hall is somewhat narrower, for a total of just over 300 square feet per apartment.

Figure 20. Original multi-paneled apartment door on the first floor of 97 Orchard Street, 2005. Photography by Andrew S. Dolkart.

The front entrance door of 97 Orchard Street and similar tenements opened into a small vestibule with an inexpensive white marble wainscot. A vestibule door led into a hall with wooden bead-molding wainscot, plaster walls and ceiling, and an Italianate style plaster arch supported on foliate brackets (Fig. 19). Each apartment was entered through a solid wood door divided into four panels. The only unaltered original apartment door extant in the building is the one leading into the front apartment on the north side of the first floor (Fig. 20). Above each door is a glazed operable transom that allowed a little light and air to filter from the apartments into the hall.

Apartments on the upper floors were reached by an unlit wood stair with a heavy newel post and railing with turned balusters that ran through the center of the building (Fig. 21). Although the stair treads were replaced several times as they wore down from the friction of thousands of feet, the original newel post and railing were always salvaged and remain in place.[24] One entered an apartment directly from the hall into the kitchen, a windowless space in the center of the unit that originally lacked cupboards, a sink, and other typical kitchen equipment. The largest room in each apart-

Figure 21. Stair at 97 Orchard Street with original newel post and railing and replacement treads with cast-iron guards, 1988. Courtesy of Lower East Side Tenement Museum.

ment was the parlor or living room, generally referred to by residents simply as the "front room." This was the only room in each apartment with exterior windows, opening either onto the street or the rear yard. Analysis of the layers of paint in the front rooms revealed wood baseboards, chair rails, and door and window frames with crude, light-tone oak graining that was part of the original decor.[25] Each front room also apparently had a wooden closet, although its configuration was changed at a later date. The presence of a closet was notable in the 1860s, since closets were still relatively rare in American domestic interiors; wardrobes were preferred for the storage of clothing.[26] On the other side of the kitchen was a tiny inner bedroom with no exterior windows.

Figure 22. Light blue distemper paint is clearly evident on the wall above the sinks.

Rooms in the tenement were originally finished with a lime-rich plaster mixed with goat and horse hair.[27] In the 1860s the walls and ceilings were painted with distemper, an inexpensive, water-based paint that could easily be washed off in preparation for the application of a new coat or a new color. While wealthy homeowners may have had their painters remove old distemper layers, tenement owners and residents did not. Thus, at 97 Orchard Street pastel shades of light blue, light green, and salmon pink distemper survive on walls, while light blue appears on ceilings and lavender blue on bedroom walls and ceilings (Fig. 22).[28] Floors were made of pine boards which were occasionally painted, at least around the perimeters of the parlors. Evidence regarding painted floors in other rooms is inconclusive, since the original paint has worn off over the years and many of the floorboards have been replaced.[29]

Since light entered apartments only through windows in the front room, the individual units were extremely dark, with forty of the sixty rooms on the five residential floors receiving no direct light. Although gas for lighting was available on Orchard Street in the 1860s, Lucas Glockner did not install it in his building, presumably because of cost. The front room opened either onto noisy, densely crowded Orchard Street or onto the shallow backyard, with the rear wall of a building on Allen Street only a few yards away. The kitchen, one room away from the windows, and the bedroom, two rooms away, received very little direct light or air.

Light and air filtered from the front room into the kitchen either via

Figure 23. Casement window between the public hall and an apartment bedroom; the iron bars, protecting the apartment from burglars, are original, 2005. Photograph by Andrew S. Dolkart.

the doorway between the rooms, when the original multi-paneled door was ajar, or through a glass transom above. Ventilation in the inner bedrooms, which measured a mere seventy square feet, was particularly problematic— a condition which housing reformers decried as being life-threatening. An 1857 *Report of the Conditions of Tenant Houses in New York* complained that inner bedrooms were "completely shut off from fresh air. In the summer, in the absence of a breeze, the air in the tenement bedroom became stagnant; in the winter, when doors, windows and other outlets were closed, the dry stove or the smoky chimney added further pollutants to an atmosphere already poisoned by the accumulated odors of natural secretions and other sources of filth."[30] Not only were the inner bedrooms far from any source of ventilation but, unlike the kitchen-parlor doorway, the doorway between the kitchen and bedroom did not have a transom. A small casement window protected by bars was cut into the wall between each inner bedroom and the hall (Fig. 23), but its purpose was probably to allow some light to flicker into the dark hall rather than to ventilate the bedroom. Indeed, there was almost no ventilation in the hall or on the stairs except when the front or rear doors on the first floor were opened; the only light in the halls emanated from the apartments through the transoms above the apartment doorways and the small casements in the bedroom walls.

What ventilation managed to reach the inner bedrooms at 97 Orchard Street came through a window opening measuring approximately 3'-8" by 4'-10" cut into the walls between the inner bedrooms and kitchens of each apartment (Fig. 24). These openings were composed of a horizontal sliding sash made up of two sliders, each glazed with three panes of glass. Evidence from an examination of early layers of paint suggest that these openings are probably original.[31] These interior windows did not permit much light to enter the inner bedrooms, but probably did improve air circulation. The presence of these windows in a building erected in 1863–64 is significant, since they were not legally required until 1903.

Water and sewer facilities at 97 Orchard Street were crude. Pipes delivering fresh water from the Croton Aqueduct had already been installed beneath Orchard Street in 1863, but the law did not require that building owners hook into this system. The 1864 survey of the Council of Hygiene and Public Health recorded that in many of the area's new five- and six-story tenements there was "Croton-water upon each floor, with sinks for ordinary slops."[32] In this respect, 97 Orchard Street was not even up to the minimal standards of other tenements, since there was no water available inside the building. Many tenements had a hydrant connected to the Croton system in the rear yard; although no evidence survives, this was probably how water was provided to tenants at 97 Orchard Street and a hydrant was reconstructed in the backyard in 2010. Tenants would have filled buckets and basins, and hauled them to their apartments.

Sewer pipes were laid beneath Orchard Street in 1863, shortly after a contract was let by the Croton Aqueduct Department for the installation of 380 feet of pipe on Orchard Street between Delancey and Broome Streets.[33] With new sewer pipes on Orchard Street, it would have been possible for Lucas Glockner to have provided indoor water closets. Indoor toilets, however, were still rare in New York City in the 1860s and were unheard of in tenements. Nevertheless, Glockner did provide toilet facilities that, however primitive, were more advanced than those required by law. Rather than creating outhouses with privy pits that would need to be periodically cleaned out, a type of primitive toilet facility that was still common in New York City in the 1860s, archaeological evidence indicates that Glockner provided his tenants (and his family, since he was an original resident) with a privy vault—an outdoor toilet or group of toilets with a common brick waste

Figure 24. Window with horizontal sliding sash, located in the wall between the kitchen and inner bedroom of an apartment as 97 Orchard Street, 2005. Photograph by Andrew S. Dolkart.

compartment that was connected to a sewer.[34] These flushable privy vaults were later referred to as "school sinks" (Figs. 25 and 26).

The vault, probably built by laborers rather than purchased from a dealer, was constructed of tightly sealed brick and was connected to the sewer running beneath Orchard Street by an eight-inch pipe that entered the building's cellar at its northwest corner.[35] The privy vault had a mechanism

Figure 25. Toilet compartments in the yard of a Lower East Side tenement, ca. 1905. Courtesy of The Irma and Paul Milstein Division of United States, Local History and Genealogy (Tenement House Commission Collection), The New York Public Library, Astor Lenox and Tilden Foundations.

with which a building janitor or housekeeper could regularly flush out the waste. Ideally the vault would be flushed daily by the building's janitor, but as tenement reformers reported later in the nineteenth century this was not always done, since "the process is a disagreeable and foul one and the stench excessive."[36] The water for flushing the privy vaults at tenements such as that at 97 Orchard Street probably came from a backyard hydrant provided with Croton water, for which Glockner, as owner of the building, would have paid an annual fee.[37]

The nine-foot length of the vault's interior could have accommodated a single row of four wood toilet compartments, each measuring about 2'-6" wide and 3'-9" deep. They were located on the north side of the lot, running along the lot line between numbers 97 and 99, and probably abutting another group of toilet compartments in the yard of number 99. Each compartment had a wood seat and a door with some sort of slit or hole for light and ventilation. The fact that the archaeological dig at 97 Orchard Street uncovered

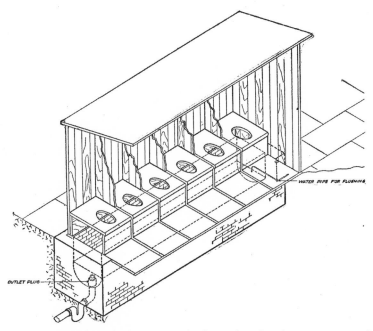

Figure 26. Diagram of school sinks or privy vaults, showing line of wooden compartments and seats, brick vault, water pipe for flushing, and plugged outlet pipe, 1903. William De Forest and Lawrence Veiller, eds., *The Tenement House Problem* (1903). Courtesy of Andrew S. Dolkart.

a broken chamber pot indicates that residents did not always choose to use these small compartments.[38] Although these toilet facilities were relatively primitive and did not meet the middle-class standards of the day, they were probably more advanced than the facilities that had been available to the immigrant tenement residents in Germany and elsewhere in Europe. Whether Glockner's installation of a flushable privy vault connected to the sewer system rather than a simple privy pit was unusual for a tenement in the 1860s cannot be determined, since no survey discusses this issue and there have been no other archaeological investigations of the rear-yard toilets in contemporaneous tenements. Such vaults may not, however, have been that rare, since Council of Hygiene and Public Health inspector J. T. Kennedy noted that the Tenth Ward was quite sanitary and that sewerage was "very complete."[39]

Tenants were supposed to place their garbage in garbage boxes set in front of the building, but these boxes were "not at all sufficient for the people disposed to be cleanly."[40] Even when they were available, they often proved to be less than ideal, as reported in a somewhat melodramatic manner, in the *New York Tribune* in 1863:

> In front of each of these tenement blocks is placed a garbage-box, which is only another name for a receptacle of heterogeneous filth and corruption, composed of potato-peelings, cabbage-heads, turnips, dead lobsters, oyster-shells, night-soil, rancid butter, dead dogs and cats, and ordinary black street mud, all forming one festering, rotting, loathsome, hellish mass of air poisoning, death-breeding filth, reeking in the fierce sunshine, which gloats yellowly over it like the glare of a devil whom Satan has kicked from his councils in virtuous disgust.[41]

Heat inside the apartments at 97 Orchard Street was provided by a stove in the kitchen, despite the presence of a fireplace in the front room of each apartment. The fireplace had a cast-iron firebox frame with a patent date of 1862, a slate hearthstone, and a simple, classically inspired wooden mantel with shallow pilasters supporting a tall frieze capped by a modest cornice (Fig. 27). Many of the fireplaces also had wooden shutters that could be closed when the fireplace was not in use to keep out drafts; others had enclosure boards.[42] The fireplaces and their mantels may have been placed in the front rooms because the traditional focal point of a parlor, even one planned for poor immigrants, was a "homey" fireplace. There were also originally fireplaces with cast-iron fireboxes and hearthstones (larger than those in the front room) in the kitchens. It is unknown if these fireplaces also had mantels, although at some point shallow mantel shelves were placed above some and possibly all of the fireboxes. All of the kitchen fireplaces were filled in during the late nineteenth century. The large hearthstones easily supported cast-iron stoves that burned either wood or coal (Fig. 28).[43]

Although all of the apartments were small and had few amenities, some apartments were more desirable than others and rents were set accordingly. A list of tenement rents compiled by Lawrence Veiller in 1900 for the block bounded by Canal, Bayard, Chrystie, and Forsyth Streets records that rents in tenements similar to 97 Orchard Street increased with the number of rooms and decreased as one ascended in a building. In addition, apartments that faced the street were better lit and thus were more expensive than those that looked onto the yard. For example, at 5 Forsyth Street, three rooms on the first floor rented for $12.00 to $13.00 per month, while on the fourth floor a similar apartment rented for $9.50 to $10.00 per month. At 13 Forsyth Street, a two-room apartment rented for $7.50 on the first floor and

Figure 27. Typical parlor fireplace and mantel at 97 Orchard Street, ca. 2000. Courtesy of Lower East Side Tenement Museum.

$6.50 to $7.00 on the third floor.[44] A similar distribution of rents was undoubtedly in effect in the 1860s when the apartments at 97 Orchard Street were first rented.

In the crowded apartments at 97 Orchard Street and other tenements erected in the second half of the nineteenth century, it is difficult to assign exact uses to each room. Since households of seven or more people were not unusual, most rooms had multiple uses. Clearly the kitchen, living room/parlor (front room), and bedroom were not limited to the same uses in tenements as in middle-class homes. In general, the kitchen, where cooking and other household tasks were completed, was also the room where family members and visitors congregated. With large households, every room could be used as a bedroom. Henry Rosenthal remembers that as a child at 97 Orchard Street early in the twentieth century, his parents slept in

Figure 28. Women sitting beside a cast-iron stove making lace in the kitchen of a tenement apartment. Photograph by Lewis W. Hines, 1911. Courtesy of Library of Congress, Prints & Photographs Division, National Child Labor Committee Collection.

the inner bedroom, his two sisters, Ida and Bessie, used a folding cot in the kitchen, and that he and his three brothers, Morris, Sam, and Phillip (then all sharing the surname Rogarshevsky) slept in the front room, with their heads on a couch and their bodies on chairs.[45] In the 1910s, the six children of Abraham and Rachel Confino, Sephardic Jewish immigrants from Kastoria, Turkey, also used the front room of their fifth-floor apartment as a bedroom—their daughter had a bed, while their five sons slept on crates softened with thick Turkish rugs called *mantas*.[46] In contrast, in the 1920s, Morris and Rebecca (Beckie) Abrams, Greek Jews from Janina, slept in the front room. Indeed, in 1925, Beckie gave birth to their son Albert in this room on a large brass bed that was the room's "main piece of furniture, along with several odd chairs." The Abrams's two daughters shared the back bedroom, while Morris's mother Sophie slept on a folding cot in the kitchen.[47] Josephine Baldizzi recalls that her Italian-immigrant parents also slept in the front room, while she and her younger brother slept in the inner bedroom; they shared a single folding bed that was, she recalled, "like a sandwich . . . you pick it up and you clip it." Her mother covered it with a cloth during the day "so it wouldn't look ugly."[48]

Figure 29. Tenement sweatshop, photographed by Jacob Riis, ca. 1889. Courtesy of Library of Congress, Prints & Photographs Division.

In some apartments, rooms were also used as home factories or sweatshops, exacerbating the problems of overcrowding (Fig. 29). The manufacture of garments (coats, dresses, shirts, caps, suspenders, and other items) was the most common type of industry in tenement apartments. However, by the end of the nineteenth century and in the early years of the twentieth century, fewer tenement factories actually manufactured clothing. Instead, coats and trousers sewn in loft factories were brought to tenements for finishing.[49] In addition to clothing, factories producing cigars, artificial flowers, mattresses, and other products were also found in the neighborhood.[50]

The presence of factories in tenement apartments was extremely controversial, not only because working conditions were often abysmal, but also because many feared epidemics. Although there was no evidence that any disease had been caused by garments manufactured in tenement factories, the fear remained that diphtheria, smallpox, chicken pox, phthisis, cholera, scarlet fever, measles, and even the plague could be carried by clothing from tenements to consumers.[51] As James Connolly, the Factory Inspector for New York State, alleged in 1892:

The garments which they handle are widely distributed, and are, so competent hygienic authorities say, the most perfect carriers of disease germs. The appearance of Asiatic cholera in one "sweat shop" may expose thousands of people, remote from the locality, to the disease. The ever-present poverty of the workers, as well as their inherent objection to making their stricken condition known, may, in case of epidemic, result in giving the plague such a start that the most extraordinary vigilance on the part of the health authorities will hardly suffice to stamp out the disease.[52]

As a result of these fears, and not as part of an effort to improve the lives and labor conditions of workers, in 1892 the New York State Legislature amended the factory law of 1886 to ban the manufacturing of coats, vests, trousers, knee-pants, overalls, cloaks, fur, fur trimming, fur garments, shirts, purses, feathers, artificial flowers, and cigars in tenement apartments without written permission.[53] The only exception was for tenements in which all workers were members of the immediate family. This exception was the result of a Court of Appeals case several years earlier that had permitted a cigar factory to remain open where all workers were family members.[54]

Even with this law regulating tenement manufacturing, hundreds of factories continued to operate, including several at 97 Orchard Street that manufactured dresses, brooms and window brushes, and cigars.[55] This may only be a fraction of the factories actually operating at 97 Orchard, since many were short-lived or escaped notice by the factory inspectors. Others might never have been surveyed since there were often not enough inspectors to survey adequately.[56] At least one factory did business at 97 Orchard Street for several years. Harris and Jennie Levine immigrated from Plonsk, Poland, in 1890 and by 1892 had moved into 97 Orchard Street, where Harris ran a dress factory employing two women and one man.[57] The women probably did much of the sewing, along with Harris, while their male employee pressed the finished garments with heavy irons heated on the kitchen stove. The dress factory was still in business in 1895, when an inspector made a return visit, then employing only two women.[58] Thus, the Levines' apartment served as both a factory and their family home. It was there that Jennie Levine raised her children and, in fact, gave birth to her third child, Max. Jennie must have competed with the presser for use of the stove where she would have cooked meals for her family and for the workers, who were in the apartment for at least ten hours per day.[59]

No evidence survives explaining whether Harris Levine legally maintained a factory in the family's tenement apartment. Harris may have had a permit, or it is also possible that Harris's employees refused to answer questions or told the inspector that they were family members. They knew, of course, that if the factory were found to be operating illegally they would lose their jobs. Harris and his workers may have been unable to communicate with the factory inspector; they may not have spoken English or may have feigned ignorance of the language. A factory inspector noted in his report for 1900 that "the real, and many times assumed, ignorance of our language among license holders and applicants for licenses, renders it most difficult to get true and reliable information regarding workrooms. . . . The inability of the tenement workers to furnish intelligent information oftentimes makes it necessary for our inspectors to depend entirely upon observation."[60]

In 1899, the law regulating tenement factories was strengthened. Although it did not wipe out these factories, it made them increasingly difficult to run. By the early years of the twentieth century, as the entire garment manufacturing process became more centralized in factories, most garment manufacturing had moved into loft buildings. The new lofts, built on the Lower East Side or on and just off Broadway between about Canal Street and 23rd Street in what are now SoHo, NoHo, and the Ladies' Mile, were all within walking distance of the labor force concentrated in Lower East Side tenements.

On the densely populated Lower East Side, crowding was not limited to the interiors of tenement apartments. On hot nights, tenement residents might have slept on the fire escapes or on the roof of their building. In fact, during the record-breaking heat wave of July 1905, doctors recommended the roof as a good place to sleep, although, as the *New York Times* recorded, "at sunrise the children of the great east side tenement districts, as well as their elders, deserted the roofs where they had spent the night, and which fairly scorched under the first rays of the sun."[61] The roof was not just used for sleeping, but was also a popular location for all types of socializing. Josephine Baldizzi recalls eating on the roof of 97 Orchard Street.[62] Seymour (Sam) Gottesman, born at 97 Orchard Street in 1901, recalls how the roof served as a social space where residents shared the latest news and gossip: "Sometimes we'd sit up on the roof. . . . that was the promised land. When you went there you had the sun. And neighbors used to get together and schmooze over politics, and settle arguments, and gossip of course. . . . The roof was the verbal newspaper. You didn't need to buy one."[63]

The streets on the Lower East Side also teemed with people. Hundreds of thousands of residents walked to and from their jobs, shopped, played in the streets, and, in many cases, worked on the streets. In 1917, travel writer Robert Shackleton described the streets of the Lower East Side as the "club house of the tenements" where the tenement population congregated on all but the coldest and wettest days.[64] The streets were not only crowded with people, but, until they were banned by Mayor Fiorello H. LaGuardia on December 1, 1938, were filled with the pushcarts from which immigrant peddlers made a living selling all types of inexpensive food, clothing, and household goods (Fig. 30). To outsiders who wrote about what they often referred to as "the ghetto":

> The streets are crowded with push carts, the walks littered with stands and baskets from which the vendors sell their wares, and a pushing, clamoring mass of humanity—women with their market baskets, crying children and babies, and here and there a man forcing his way through the mass while the women and peddlers hurl imprecations at him—form a scene of confusion which has no counterpart in the world.[65]

Josephine Baldizzi remembers the peddlers outside the window of her apartment calling:

> a nickel and a dime
> rain or shine
> any time
> a nickel and a dime.[66]

Figure 30. Pushcart market on Orchard Street north of Delancey Street, photographed by Ewing Galloway, ca. 1910. Courtesy of The Irma and Paul Milstein Division of United States, Local History and Genealogy (New York City Street Views), The New York Public Library, Astor Lenox and Tilden Foundations.

NEW TENEMENT LAWS AND THE CHANGING CHARACTER OF THE LOWER EAST SIDE AND ITS TENEMENTS

As the number of tenements increased in New York City, expanding the boundaries of immigrant neighborhoods, laws were enacted that not only regulated tenement construction, but also sought to improve the lives of residents. The first law that had any effect on existing tenements such as 97 Orchard Street was the Tenement House Act of 1867; this was also the first law to define the word "tenement." The law was passed as a result of the Council of Hygiene and Public Health's 1865 report and the council's pleas for reform.[1] Although the provisions of this law were weak and often ignored by many owners, the bill succeeded in establishing a precedent for government regulation of conditions in tenement houses. Laws enacted in succeeding decades, in contrast, had a profound influence on the design of new tenements and the improvement of living conditions in older buildings.

The 1867 act mandated that one toilet or privy be provided for every twenty people, that privies be connected to sewers where these were available, and that a three-foot-square transom be provided over the doors of all interior bedrooms. Other provisions required fire escapes, banisters on hall stairs, minimum ceiling heights, and banned animals (except for dogs and cats) in residential buildings.

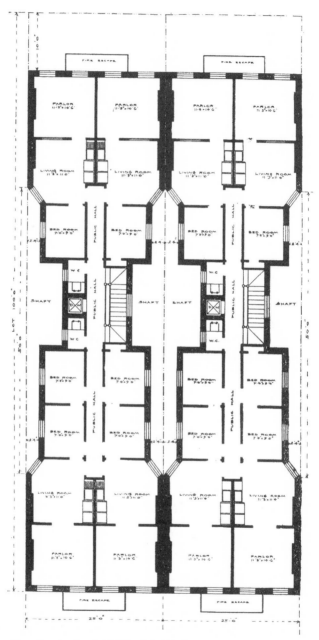

Figure 31. Plan of a pair of typical "old law," dumbbell tenements. *First Report of the Tenement House Department of the City of New York,* vol. 1 (1903). Courtesy of Andrew S. Dolkart.

Although these provisions had an impact on many tenements, they did not affect 97 Orchard Street, since the privies at 97 Orchard Street were already connected to a sewer (although if there were actually four privy compartments, as the museum believes, they served more than twenty people each) and the requirement for transoms was never complied with. Glockner could not have added these transoms, since there was no room above the doors. He was probably able to ignore this requirement of the law because he had already provided a window in the wall between these two rooms.

Demands by reformers for improvements in the laws governing the design of new tenements continued into the 1870s, especially as speculative tenement construction increased late in the decade when the real estate industry recovered from the 1873 national depression. Little resulted from reformers' campaigns. James Ford notes that "it was not lack of recognition of the problem, but rather lack of vision, courage, or persistency, and skill in reform politics, that permitted the evils of congested living to become so deeply rooted in the life and thought-habits of the people."[2] Efforts at reform finally resulted in the passage of the Tenement House Act of 1879 (often referred to as the "old law").[3] This law was inspired by an 1878 competition in the magazine *Plumber and Sanitary Engineer* that sought ideas for an economical model tenement on the typical twenty-five foot wide lot. The winning scheme by architect James E. Ware was for a building with narrow shafts in the center. In shape, the plan resembled that of a dumbbell weight. The law passed by the state legislature required that all rooms have windows facing the street, rear yard, or an interior shaft. The most common design resulting from this requirement was the "dumbbell," similar to that proposed by Ware (Fig. 31).[4] These dumbbell tenements, and those with similar shaft designs, are also referred to as "old law" tenements. Unfortunately, the shafts required by the 1879 law were so small that they provided little light and air to apartments below the top floor; instead, they became receptacles for garbage and created flues that sucked flames from one floor to another during a fire. In addition, the shaft windows of adjoining apartments were so close that privacy was virtually eliminated.[5] Soon after the dumbbell plan was first suggested, a *New York Times* editorial noted that if the dumbbell was the best solution to the city's housing problem, then "the problem is unsolvable."[6] Even the judges for the *Plumber and Sanitary Engineer* competition who chose Ware's design were unhappy with the result, stating that "in their view it is impossible to secure the requirements of physical and moral health" on narrow city lots.[7] The law only regulated new construction, having no effect on pre-existing tenements; it did, however, succeed in prohibiting the construction of buildings with windowless interior rooms such as 97 Orchard Street.

Until 1901, when a new tenement house act banned the construction of dumbbell tenements, many such tenements were erected on the Lower East Side. Several dozen were built on Orchard Street, including the four buildings at 101–107 (Rentz & Lange, architect, 1888) to the north of numbers 97 and 99 (Fig. 32). Although many dumbbell tenements were built in the Tenth Ward, they were never as numerous there as in other tenement areas; this ward had already been heavily developed with tenements prior to 1879, leaving fewer development sites. Larger concentrations of dumbbell tenements are found in Yorkville and East Harlem, two uptown areas that underwent major tenement development during the final decades of the nineteenth century.

In the 1880s, the population of the Tenth Ward changed as the Germans who had dominated this district moved to other neighborhoods, such as the East Village and Yorkville in Manhattan, and Williamsburg and Bushwick in Brooklyn. New German immigrants also chose to settle in these other neighborhoods rather than on the Lower East Side. In their place, Eastern European Jewish immigrants increasingly began to settle in the Tenth Ward. Indeed, the arrival of Jewish immigrants appears to have hastened the departure of the German residents. A survey completed in 1901 by the United States Industrial Commission describes the changes in population on the Lower East Side:

> The Hebrew population in the city already dense in 1890 . . . has increased tremendously since then. . . . On the East Side they have extended their limits remarkably within the past 10 years . . . driving the Germans before them, until it may be said that all of the East Side below Fourteenth street is a Jewish district. . . . The Germans did not like the proximity of the Jews, and so they left.[8]

The start of this trend in population change was already evident in the 1880 census, which recorded ten Russian-born residents living at 97 Orchard Street. By 1900, the census records only two German-born residents left in the building. Russian Jews made up the vast majority of inhabitants, with smaller numbers from Romania and Poland.[9] The occupations of residents also shifted, with fewer skilled artisans and far more men and women employed in the garment trades.

The changing character of the population is also evident in the owner-

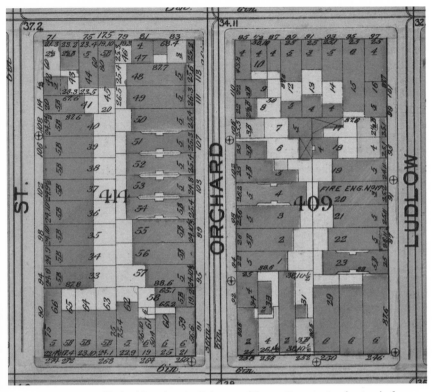

Figure 32. Map of Orchard Street between Delancey and Broome Streets in 1899 showing the four dumbbell tenements at 101–107 Orchard Street. G. W. Bromley & Company, *Atlas of the City of New York Borough of Manhattan*, vol. 1 (1899; updated to 1900). Courtesy of Avery Architectural and Fine Arts Library, Columbia University in the City of New York.

ship pattern of tenements on the Lower East Side. In the 1860s and 1870s the ethnicity of tenement owners such as Lucas Glockner reflected the dominance of German immigrants as builders, owners, and residents in the Tenth Ward. By the 1880s, however, as the German population in the ward declined, an increasing number of Eastern European Jewish immigrants purchased older tenements or erected new buildings.[10] In 1886 Lucas Glockner, who had built the tenement at 97 Orchard Street, sold the building. Over the next few decades, a succession of Jewish immigrants bought and sold 97 Orchard Street, many retaining the building for only a short time.[11] A similar if less dramatic shift in ownership occurred in the Italian Fourteenth Ward located to the west of the Bowery, with Italians owning one-quarter of the tenements on Elizabeth Street in 1905 and one half by 1925.[12]

As the population in *Kleindeutschland* changed from German to Eastern

European Jewish, the tenants in the stores on the lower floors of most tenements also shifted. Throughout the period when Lucas Glockner owned 97 Orchard Street, John Schneider ran his saloon in the basement. But in 1886, the same year that Glockner sold the building, Schneider vacated his space, relocating his saloon across the street to 98 Orchard Street. Henry Infeld, an immigrant from Austria, continued to run a saloon in the basement commercial space, but the viability of German lager beer saloons was declining in the Tenth Ward as the German population ebbed. By 1890, both Infeld's and Schneider's saloons had closed. Following the demise of Infeld's saloon in 1889, partitions were added to the commercial space in the basement of 97 Orchard Street, dividing the space into two separate stores. These were leased to Eastern European Jewish immigrants. Wolf Rudinsky, an immigrant from Russia, opened a grocery in one storefront and Galician immigrant Israel Aaron Lustgarten operated a kosher butcher shop in the other (some evidence indicates that Lustgarten occupied the north store front). Both the Rudinsky and Lustgarten families lived in the building, probably in the apartments located behind each of the stores. In 1900, Israel Lustgarten and his wife Goldie lived in the rear apartment with four of their six children and a boarder.[13]

The Lustgarten's butcher shop and family apartment remained at 97 Orchard Street until 1902 when the family relocated to Broome Street, perhaps as a result of vandalism to their store during the kosher meat boycott that spring. In May of 1902, wholesale meat dealers raised the price of kosher meat, forcing retailers to increase the cost from twelve to eighteen cents a pound, a substantial increase that was difficult for the poor Jewish consumers to absorb. Though the retail butchers had initially protested the increase, they had to accept the rise in prices. In turn, women on the Lower East Side mounted a powerful protest, holding rallies, boycotting shops, and capturing the attention of both the English and Yiddish language press. On May 16, 1902, Lustgarten's shop was the target of the protest and its front window was shattered, an event captured by a photographer for the *New York World*. Ultimately, the boycott resulted in a temporary decrease in the cost of kosher meat.[14]

Apartments at 97 Orchard Street and those in thousands of other tenements were also extensively altered in the late nineteenth and early twentieth centuries in response to new laws, changing lifestyles, and the filtering down of new technologies to housing for the poor. Many of these changes were purely cosmetic, such as new types and colors of paint or new wallpaper and floor coverings. For example, while pastel-colored distemper paint was common in the earliest years of tenement occupancy, by the 1880s American paint companies had introduced new products and new colors—most importantly, longer-lasting, ready-mixed oil-based paint. At 97 Orchard Street oil-based orange, pink, and red-brown paints are found in parlors and blues and greens are found in the kitchens and bedrooms in the 1880s. In the late 1890s, blue and green continued to be popular in the bedrooms and kitchens, but the parlor walls were papered. Woodwork continued to be crudely grained, although the graining color became darker. By the 1920s, cream and yellow became the most common paint colors and the woodwork was painted cream or white.[15] The consistency of paint colors from one apartment to another leads to the conclusion that it was the landlord who supplied the paint.[16]

Figure 33. Layers of wallpaper on a parlor wall. Photograph by Lower East Side Tenement Museum 2011.

In addition, wallpaper began to replace paint in parlors, probably in the late 1880s or early 1890s. Inexpensive, mass-produced wallpapers, often printed on cheap pulp papers, were widely available by the late nineteenth century; an entire tenement apartment could be papered for a few dollars or, at four cents a roll and entire tenement apartments could be papered for less than one dollar.[17] Layers of wallpaper survive in many tenement parlors (Fig. 33) in spite of an 1895 law mandating that "no wall paper shall be placed upon a wall or ceiling of any tenement or lodging-house, unless all paper shall be first removed therefrom and said wall and ceiling thoroughly cleaned."[18] This law was enacted as a result of reform campaigns based on the belief that the layers of wallpaper glue attracted vermin.[19] Owners and tenants, however, apparently saw no need to undertake the laborious job of stripping earlier layers of paper. Wallpaper patterns included popular nineteenth- and twentieth-century floral (Fig. 34), striped, and scrollwork patterns and even inexpensive papers with bronze or silver highlights; many papered walls were further accented with boldly patterned, often contrasting border papers.[20]

Figure 34. Floral wallpaper found at 97 Orchard Street, ca. 2000. Courtesy of Lower East Side Tenement Museum (photograph by Reba Fishman Snyder).

The type of floor coverings used by residents also changed over time. Early tenants placed inexpensive rugs on the wooden floors. In the 1910s, affordable linoleum became available and was used in many kitchens and parlors. Linoleum was invented in England in about 1860 by Frederick Walton, who combined linseed oil with cork or sawdust and other materials and then spread the liquid on a backing of burlap or canvas in an effort to create a durable floor surface. In 1872, Walton established an American factory on Staten Island, New York, in an area that came to be known as Linoleumville (now Travis). Linoleum became popular because it was high decorative, easy to maintain, soft on the feet, considered to be sanitary, and, most significantly, was inexpensive. By the early twentieth century, several firms were manufacturing linoleum in the United States in a wide variety of patterns.[21] The patterns chosen by residents at 97 Orchard Street ranged from imitation Persian and Chinese rugs (Fig. 35) to modernist geometric abstractions (Fig. 36). Remnants of several layers of linoleum are extant in some rooms since, as with wallpaper, tenants did not always remove the older covering when laying a new sheet. In addition, as the linoleum wore out in one spot, such as at entrance portals or near sinks, it was often patched with a new and unrelated pattern.

The public hallways in tenements such as 97 Orchard Street were sub-

Figure 35. Linoleum with a Persian rug design found on an apartment floor at 97 Orchard Street, ca. 2000. Courtesy of Lower East Side Tenement Museum.

Figure 36. Linoleum with a geometric design found on an apartment floor at 97 Orchard Street, 2005. Photograph by Andrew S. Dolkart.

ject to an enormous amount of wear. A *Real Estate Record* article from 1901 described "bare boards worn into hollows by the tramping of many feet, with pine-knots sticking out of the surface now and then like a miniature mountain."²² In about 1905, the floor of the entrance vestibule and first-floor hallway at 97 Orchard Street were redesigned, adding extremely durable but inexpensive white hexagonal ceramic tiles framed by a border of red square tiles and a decorative fret pattern of blue square tiles (see Fig. 19). The wood stairs also deteriorated rapidly from the friction created by hundreds of people climbing up and down each day and, as a result, the treads had to be replaced several times. In the final early twentieth-century replacement, cast-iron tread guards were installed to forestall further deterioration (see Fig. 21).

Figure 37. Scenic roundel painted ca. 1905 on the burlap wall covering of the first-floor hall of 97 Orchard Street, ca. 2000. Courtesy of Lower East Side Tenement Museum.

Changes were also made to the walls and ceilings of the hallways as they deteriorated. The walls of the hall on the first floor of 97 Orchard Street were redesigned in an elaborate manner, probably in 1905, at the same time that the new floor was installed. The most significant change to the walls was the addition of an inexpensive but durable wall covering of burlap dyed red (the burlap was later painted a white or off-white). Burlap was a popular material for wall coverings in the early twentieth century because it was inexpensive, durable, and could easily be painted.[23] In the hall at 97 Orchard Street, the edges of the burlap and the joints created where the sheets of burlap meet were covered with mass-produced, gold-leafed, composite bead-and-reel moldings (see Fig. 19).[24] After the burlap was applied, the new wall covering was painted with landscape scenes in roundels (Fig. 37), and three-dimensional plaster arabesques that appear to have been applied on site with a device similar to a cake icer were also added. Romantic paintings and swirling arabesques may seem incongruous in the hall of an overcrowded tenement, but this type of decor, while never common, was not unique to 97 Orchard Street (Fig. 38).[25] This colorful burlap wall covering hid deteriorated plaster walls, making the property more appealing to potential commercial tenants and their customers, and to potential residential tenants in the competitive and extremely lucrative tenement real estate business.

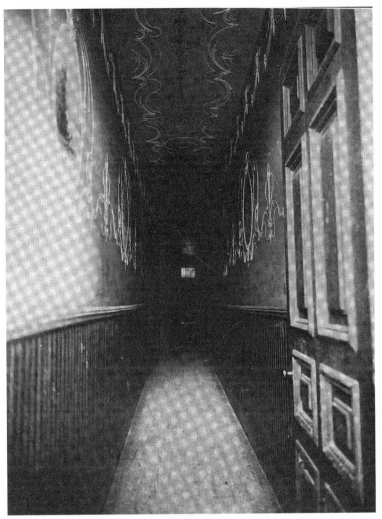

Figure 38. Unidentified tenement hallway with wall coverings and decoration similar to those at 97 Orchard Street, ca. 1907. *Fourth Report of the Tenement House Department of New York* (1907). Courtesy of William Dailey.

Many owners installed easily maintained sheets of pressed metal over deteriorated plaster in public areas. Pressed metal, especially for ceiling use, became popular in the United States in the last decades of the nineteenth century because it was fireproof, durable, decorative, and inexpensive. Despite being commonly identified as tin ceilings, they are actually more typically made of iron. Many companies manufactured the pressed-metal

Figure 39. Pressed-metal ceiling in the hall at 97 Orchard Street, ca. 2000. Courtesy of Lower East Side Tenement House Committee exhibition. William De Forest and Lawrence Veiller, eds., *The Tenement House Problem* (1903). Courtesy of Lower East Side Tenement Museum. Photograph by Michael Lillard.

sheets using a wide array of geometric and organic patterns that could be applied to walls as well as to ceilings. Once installed, the metal sheets would have been painted just as if they were plaster. At number 97, the pressed-metal ceilings in the halls (Fig. 39) were installed relatively early in the history of the building, perhaps in the 1870s or early 1880s, evident from the fact that there are only three layers of paint on the original plasterwork underneath. Pressed metal was also installed on the hallway walls, but probably not until shortly after 1905. The hallway walls have nine layers of paint covered by a layer of dark red burlap. Since the fabric shows no evidence of dirt or wear, it was probably installed just before the pressed metal. Different patterns of pressed metal are visible in the halls of 97 Orchard Street, since sections were often patched with a piece of metal that did not match the original.[26]

5

THE 1901 TENEMENT HOUSE ACT AND THE TENEMENT HOUSE DEPARTMENT

The alarming deterioration of the overcrowded tenement districts of New York City in the late nineteenth century spurred middle-class progressive reformers to press for passage of reform legislation. In 1896, the *New York Times* summarized reformers' concerns:

> The chief objections to the old-style tenements are contracted quarters, lack of family privacy, and promiscuous toilet arrangements, inviting moral deterioration; lack of light and air, and of sanitary accommodations, insuring a large death rate, and danger from fire—that ever-present tenement horror. All of these are wickedly cruel when such houses are new; when they become old, dilapidated, infested with vermin and infected with disease germs, they are a disgrace to humanity and a menace, not only to the health of the unfortunate residents therein, but to the health of the whole community.[1]

Under the leadership of Lawrence Veiller and the Charity Organization Society of the City of New York (COS), the movement to improve tenement conditions intensified in the late 1890s and first months of the new century. Veiller believed that "bad tenement house conditions were the cause of most of the problems in our modern cities."[2] He

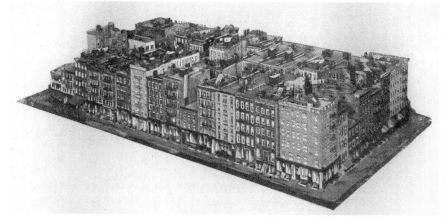

Figure 40. Model of the block bounded by Chrystie, Forsyth, Bayard, and Canal Streets displayed at the 1900 Tenement House Committee exhibition. William De Forest and Lawrence Veiller, eds., *The Tenement House Problem* (1903). Courtesy of Andrew S. Dolkart.

proposed that the COS establish an organization that would seek to improve conditions in tenement houses by securing remedial legislation regulating new construction, assuring that existing laws were enforced, stimulating the construction of model tenements, and improving conditions in older tenements.[3]

Veiller's proposal led to the founding of the Tenement House Committee of the COS in 1899. The committee unsuccessfully sought to influence a city commission that was recommending changes to the building code.[4] The building code commission's recommendations, which became law in October 1899, actually made conditions worse: permitting, for example, eight-story tenements and wooden tenements for six families, which had previously been illegal.[5] This setback convinced the committee that "no real progress in tenement house reform was to be made unless the whole community was aroused to a knowledge of existing conditions."[6] With this in mind, the committee organized an exhibition "as a means of bringing the attention of the community to the condition of tenement houses in New York City and in other large cities of the country and Europe."[7] The exhibition, which took place in February 1900 in the former Sherry Building on Fifth Avenue and East 37th Street, included photographs, maps, charts, and models graphically illustrating the overcrowding, poverty, and disease in the tenement house districts.[8] Perhaps the most dramatic exhibit was a pair of models: one was of the buildings on the Lower East Side block bounded

Figure 41. Model illustrating the density of a block if it were built up entirely with dumbbell tenements, displayed at the 1900 Tenement House Committee exhibition. William De Forest and Lawrence Veiller, eds., *The Tenement House Problem* (1903). Courtesy of Andrew S. Dolkart.

by Christie, Forsyth, Bayard, and Canal Streets which housed 2,781 people (Fig. 40), and the other was of a hypothetical block, built up entirely with dumbbell tenements on narrow lots, that could have housed 4,000 people (Fig. 41).[9] The exhibition was visited by more than 10,000 people during its two-week run, and it introduced its largely middle-class audience to the conditions that reformers thought needed to be changed in tenement districts.

The exhibition led the New York State Legislature to pass a bill empowering Governor Theodore Roosevelt to appoint a tenement-house commission "to make a careful examination into the tenement houses in cities of the first class [i.e., New York City and Buffalo]; their condition as to construction, healthfulness, safety, rentals, and the effect of tenement-house life on the health, education, savings, and morals of those who live in tenement houses; and all other phases of the so-called tenement-house question in these cities that can affect public welfare."[10] The commission was presented with an extraordinarily broad mandate to investigate all aspects of tenement construction and the lives of those who lived in these buildings. Governor Roosevelt strongly supported tenement reform efforts. He had, in fact, been the principal speaker at the opening of the Tenement House Committee's exhibition. In announcing the appointment of the Tenement Commission in April 1900, Roosevelt declared, "this Tenement House Commission is the most important commission I have had to deal with . . . for it deals with one of the great fundamental factors in the most difficult and most complex of the social and industrial problems of the day."[11] He appointed a large commission with members representing many pertinent fields of interest including builders, architects, lawyers, administrators, and philanthropists. Most, however, were already advocates for reform—including, for example, Robert W. DeForest, president of the Charity Organization Society; former New York City Health Commissioner Dr. George B. Fowler; Dr. E. R. L. Gould, president of the City and Suburban Homes Company, builders of model tenements; architect and social reformer I. N. Phelps Stokes; and Alfred T. White, president of the Brooklyn Bureau of Charities and patron of several pioneering model tenement complexes.[12]

The commission heard testimony from many experts on tenements and also went on several inspection tours to tenement districts of the city. They decided to focus their study on a few typical blocks in order to ascertain whether laws in effect were actually being enforced. Specific studies were undertaken regarding tenement fires and tuberculosis, a disease seen as a special problem in overcrowded tenement districts.[13] In February 1901, the commission issued its report to the new governor, Benjamin B. Odell, Jr., who succeeded Theodore Roosevelt when he became vice president. The commission summarized the poor conditions in New York City's tenements, noting, as the *New York Times* reported, that "the most serious evils confronting the commission were insufficiency of light and air, due to narrow courts and airshafts; undue height of houses, and to the occupation by the building or adjacent buildings of too great a proportion of the lot area; danger from fire, lack of separate water closets and washing facilities, overcrowding, foul cellars and courts, and like evils, classed as bad housekeeping."[14] The commissioners recommended specific legislation that would improve conditions in tenements and tenement neighborhoods, and, significantly, proposed the establishment of a Tenement House Department authorized to assure that laws governing tenements were actually followed by builders and owners.[15]

So effective was the work of the COS and the Tenement House Commission that the State Legislature almost immediately held hearings on the proposed new laws. Although a few spoke in opposition, the speed with which the legislature acted precluded much organized opposition. The *New York Times*—not always a supporter of reform efforts—editorialized about the hearings, suggesting that opposition to the reforms was limited solely to concerns about retaining maximum profitability. It reported that the "gravest considerations of public health, decency, and morality were urged upon the one hand. Upon the other there was nothing affecting the merits of the measure but an apprehension that what has heretofore been an excessively profitable form of investment in real estate may cease to be excessively profitable."[16]

The real estate community did, indeed, oppose the law. In March 1901, the *Real Estate Record and Builders Guide*, a weekly magazine that generally expressed the interests of the real estate community, editorialized against it:

> Maintaining, as we have always done, that the solution of the tenement house problem can be found rather in encouraging the building of tenement houses than by discouraging it; and being strongly averse to any experimental increases in the public expenses at the present time, we feel compelled to oppose the bills of the Tenement House Commission.[17]

The editorial went on to decry the loss of rentable space that would result if the law were passed, warned that builders might stop developing tenements and invest their money elsewhere, suggested that the new tenements required by the law might not be marketable, and criticized the expense of establishing a tenement house department.[18]

On April 12, 1901, only two months after the commission issued its report, the Tenement House Act of 1901 was enacted.[19] The act became known as the "new law," and tenements erected after its passage are known as "new law tenements." Tenement builders were certainly aware that this law was about to pass; in early April their rush to file plans with the Department of Buildings for new tenements before the terms of the new law become effective "amazed the employes [sic] of the department by its intensity." A *New York Tribune* reporter, describing how builders "literally stormed" the department, compared the rush to submit plans to a run on a bank.[20] In an attempt to evade the provisions of the new law, some builders and architects apparently even submitted dummy plans that would later be amended. In July 1901, the Tenement House Committee accused architect Michael Bernstein, a prolific tenement designer, of submitting fifty-three false plans before the new law went into effect. The commission alleged that Bernstein had reproduced the plans for a previously built tenement that he had designed and submitted these plans for multiple new projects, many on sites of different dimensions. Bernstein, of course, vigorously denied any wrongdoing.[21]

The 1901 Tenement House Act was the most far-reaching of all the tene-ment reform bills; James Ford states that "the Tenement House Act of 1901 is the most significant regulatory act in America's history of housing."[22] The passage of this law needs to be seen in the context of a series of Progres-sive Era reforms that were efforts by middle- and upper-class Americans to improve aspects of life in the overcrowded slum districts of New York and other American cities and inculcate the residents of these areas with their values. This is evident on the Lower East Side in the construction of settle-ment houses such as the Henry Street Settlement, University Settlement, and the Educational Alliance; the expansion of the public school system where the children of immigrants could be taught American values; the establishment of trade schools such as the Hebrew Technical Institute for Girls on Henry Street, where immigrants and their children learned the skills necessary for making a living; and the creation of systems of public baths (such as that on Allen Street near Rivington Street), public libraries (such as the Seward Park Branch on East Broadway), and small parks (such as Seward Park and Hamilton Fish Park), all of which contributed to re-forming life in these densely crowded neighborhoods.[23]

Provisions of the 1901 Tenement House Act, such as increasing the size of light and air shafts for new buildings and decreasing the percentage of a lot which a building could occupy, effectively stopped the construction of tenements on twenty-five-foot-wide lots.[24] As far-reaching as these provi-sions were, they did not radically improve conditions. For example, the provisions for minimum light and air resulted in courts and shafts that were still relatively small, but which were undoubtedly an improvement over the tiny dumbbell shafts.[25] In its editorials supporting both the Tene-ment House Commission's recommendations and the new law, the *New York Tribune* complemented the commission and the state legislature for their moderation in seeking to improve housing conditions while still insur-ing that new construction would be profitable.[26]

The most important aspect of the new law for 97 Orchard Street and other older tenement buildings was that it mandated a series of changes designed to address the dangerous and unsanitary conditions in these pre-existing tenements, including mandating improved lighting, banning inner bedrooms that were two rooms away from a window, and requiring the addition of one toilet for every two families. A related law created the Tene-ment House Department to ensure implementation of the new law.[27]

Outraged real estate owners claimed, somewhat disingenuously, that the law "came unannounced and unheralded upon an unsuspecting real estate public like a thunderbolt from a clear sky," and had been "railroaded through the Legislature."[28] Opponents believed that the new law would inhibit the construction of new buildings and that the required improvements would increase an owner's expenses and lower rent rolls in older buildings. The opposition to the new law coalesced under the auspices of the United Real Estate Owners' Association, a group "composed of the various local Real Estate Owners' and Taxpayers' Associations of the City of New York, . . . organized for the purpose of safe guarding the interests of property owners."[29] In June 1901, the association established a Tenement House Committee "to oppose the restrictive and oppressive measures of the New Tenement House Law . . . [and] to test the constitutionality of its many burdensome features."[30] By July, the committee had hired a lawyer and decided that although "no attempt will be made to defeat such provisions as the lighting of halls and the ventilation requirements," other parts of the bill, especially those relating to inner bedrooms and toilets, would be vigorously opposed.[31]

On September 12, 1901, the association held its first mass meeting to condemn the new law. The large assembly room at the New York Turn Hall on Lexington Avenue and East 85th Street was, according to the *New York Times*, "packed to overflowing" as speakers derided the law for depriving them of their property without due process of the law and subjecting them to an illegal exercise of police power. To great applause, the association's president, Henry Markus, somewhat belatedly condemned the members of the Tenement House Commission as elitists who lived in affluent neighborhoods (Robert De Forest, for example, lived on Washington Square North) and knew nothing about tenements. Markus quipped that wealthy commissioner I. N. Phelps Stokes had probably never even seen a tenement. He challenged small-scale real estate owners to force changes in the law, especially to provisions relating to old tenements:

> We real estate men are opposed to a law that positively destroys property. It is a law that orders improvement in already existing tenements that are neither based on common sense nor on justice. The association must take action at once, and through the courts, for its members' protection. Astors and Goelets [two families with extensive real estate holdings] we can't get to help, but we must enlist all the smaller property holders. We must reform the reformers who gave us this law.[32]

The 1901 Tenement House Act required the alteration of old tenements in three areas: light and ventilation in public halls, light and ventilation

Figure 42. Doorway at 97 Orchard Street with wood panels replaced by figured glass in response to a requirement of the 1901 Tenement House Act, 2005. Photograph by Andrew S. Dolkart.

in apartments, and toilet facilities. The least controversial changes, those that the United Real Estate Owners' Association chose not to challenge, increased the amount of light and air in the public halls of older buildings. These provisions involved no structural alterations to the buildings. Halls had been seen as a problem for many years, since they generally received no direct natural light and seldom had adequate artificial light. In 1900, a resident of Forsyth Street who had lived in fourteen different tenements over a period of seventeen years, testified before the Tenement House Committee that the hallways "are dark in most houses that I have lived in. One tumbles over human obstacles and other obstacles, especially little children."[33]

In order to increase light in "a public hall on any floor . . . not light enough in the daytime to permit a person to read in every part thereof without the aid of artificial light," the law required that translucent glass panels be inserted into the wooden apartment doors or that a fixed sash window be cut into the partition wall between the hall and a room in each apartment that looked out onto the street, yard, or shaft.[34] At 97 Orchard Street, the upper panels were removed from the apartment doors and sheets of translucent, textured, figured glass were added (Fig. 42).[35] Another requirement of the law to increase light in the halls was the installation of a ventilating skylight with a glazed surface of not less than twenty square feet directly over the stair. A skylight that met the requirements of the 1901 law was installed at 97 Orchard Street as part of the major alterations to the building in 1905 that brought it into accord with the 1901 law.[36] Finally, the 1901 law required that a lamp was to burn from sunset to sunrise near the stair on the entrance floor and the second floor.[37] This requirement was apparently the impetus for the installation of gas lines throughout 97 Orchard Street. Gas lines are extant beneath the floors; physical evidence indicates that the floorboards were removed and channels cut in the joists for the addition of these lines. A cap on a gas pressure reduction device on the first floor is inscribed "Property of the American Gas Reduction Co., NY." This firm began business in 1896.[38] This date, coupled with evidence from paint analysis, points to circa 1905 as the date when gas was installed at 97 Orchard Street, corresponding with other major changes made at that time. Max Mason recalls that as a nine-year-old in 1921, having just arrived at 97 Orchard Street from Russia to join his father, "illumination came via gas-fed outlets lit by a match."[39] In order to turn on the gas, a tenant had to feed a coin-operated meter located in his or her apartment and then turn a gas cock and light the gas with a match. Even after gas lines were installed, kerosene lamps remained in use since not everyone could afford the twenty-five-cents-an-hour cost, and often only turned on the gas for special occasions.[40] Ironically, by the time gas was finally installed at 97 Orchard Street it was a declining technology, since electricity was rapidly replacing gas not only in the homes of more affluent people, but also in newly built tenements.

Far more controversial than lighting the halls was the banning of second interior windowless rooms. The Tenement House Department's survey found that there were "over 350,000 dark interior rooms, without any light whatsoever, that in a great majority of these rooms there are no windows at all, not even a window connecting with another room in the same apartment, [and] that many of these rooms are two rooms removed from the outer air."[41] Although these interior rooms were unpleasant places in which to sleep, they did at least provide extra space, for which tenants paid additional rent. The 1901 law allowed first interior windowless rooms in tenements, but mandated that a window be cut into the partition between an interior room, usually the kitchen, and a room with windows looking onto the street, rear yard, or an acceptable air shaft, such as a "sash window having at least fifteen square feet of glazed surface, being at least three feet high and five feet wide between stop beads, and at least one-half thereof being made to open readily."[42] As approved in 1901, the law only allowed a single interior room to be ventilated and lit in this manner. Second windowless inner rooms (e.g., the bedroom in each apartment at 97 Orchard Street) became illegal.

This ban on unventilated second interior rooms provoked fierce opposition from tenement house owners. The United Real Estate Owners'

Association took the lead in protesting this section of the law.[43] In the fall of 1901, a lively debate ensued in the pages of the *Real Estate Record* and other publications concerning the necessity of these changes, the manner in which interior bedrooms could be lit, and the expense these changes would entail.[44] Veiller suggested that the provisions of the law could be met by simply removing the wall between the kitchen and the second inner room, turning a three-room apartment into a two-room unit, with a curtain being hung in the enlarged room to divide it into two spaces.[45] Alternatively, an air shaft could be constructed that would ventilate the interior room. The construction of such a shaft, however, involved significant and costly structural change and reduced rentable space, since the shaft would cut into the already minimal square footage of each apartment.

This vocal, well-funded opposition prevailed. A 1903 amendment to the original act legalized second interior rooms as long as they had sash windows cut into partitions with other rooms.[46] A *Real Estate Record* editorial praised the "good sense of the Legislature" and suggested that owners promptly comply with this requirement.[47] 97 Orchard Street was one of the minority of older tenements that already had windows cut into the walls between the kitchen and inner bedroom, and it probably also had windows in the walls between the kitchen and parlor prior to 1901.[48] What is definitely known is that these kitchen/parlor windows had been cut through by July 10, 1902, when a tenement house inspector surveyed 97 Orchard Street and reported their presence. Unlike the horizontal sliders of the earlier kitchen-bedroom windows, the windows added between the living rooms and kitchens were double-hung, with two panes in each sash (Fig. 43).

The most important and by far most controversial change required by the 1901 law was the removal of all school sinks and privy vaults from tenement yards. The law required that "in all now existing tenement houses, all school sinks, privy vaults or other similar receptacles used to receive fecal matter, urine or sewage, shall before January first, nineteen hundred and three, be completely removed . . . [and] replaced by individual water-closets of durable non-absorbent material, properly sewer connected."[49] If necessary, the law permitted water closets in the yard, so long as they had flush tanks and were protected against frost. Whether inside or outside, one water closet was to be provided for every two families and each toilet was to be placed in a separate compartment.[50] This section of the law was to go into effect on January 1, 1903. Construction of water closets inside the tenements required substantial structural changes to old buildings, since water and sewage lines had to be installed and the space required for the water closets

Figure 43. Window cut into a wall between the kitchen and parlor of an apartment at 97 Orchard Street, ca. 2000. Courtesy of Lower East Side Tenement Museum.

had to be taken from the apartments. Although airshaft requirements for interior rooms were rescinded as a result of lobbying by building owners, the provisions for interior water closets were actually strengthened in a 1902 amendment to the law which required that each interior water closet compartment be ventilated by a window of not less than three square feet opening directly to the outer air.[51] This amendment required that if the water closets were placed in the center of each tenement floor, then air shafts had to be provided.

Most owners did not install the required toilet facilities. As a result, in 1903 the Tenement House Department brought legal action against Katie Moeschen, owner of a tenement at 332 East 39th Street, for failure to comply with the requirements of the 1901 Act. *Tenement House Department of the City of New York v. Moeschen* became the United Real Estate Owners' Association test case challenging the legality of this provision of the law.[52] An agreement was reached between the Owners' Association and the city's Corporation Counsel stipulating that the case would be framed in such a way that a final decision would apply to all buildings in the city with toilets that did not comply with the 1901 law. It was also agreed that, no matter what the decision of the Municipal Court, the case would be automatically appealed.

A jury trial was held at the Municipal Court in 1903. The defendant's lawyer asserted, among other things, that the Tenement House Act was a violation of the Fourteenth Amendment to the United States Constitution because it deprived an individual of property by imposing an unreasonable, arbitrary, improper, and unfair requirement on owners without due process of law or adequate compensation. He also claimed that the school sinks were legal since they had been installed prior to 1890 in response to an order from the Board of Health.[53] The jury at the Municipal Court held for the city. The case was appealed, first going before the New York State Supreme Court, Appellate Term, in 1903, and then to the New York State Supreme Court, Appellate Division, First Department, and finally to the New York State Court of Appeals in 1904. All decisions in the state courts were unanimous in upholding the tenement law. Finally, the case was appealed to the United States Supreme Court, which in 1906 affirmed the rulings of the New York State courts.[54] The Tenement House Department commented that the United States Supreme Court's decision was the "culmination of what is and will be about the most important litigation under the Tenement House Law. . . . Indeed the Moeschen case is a milestone in litigation relating to the enforcement of laws pertaining to health and sanitation."[55]

A few tenement owners had removed school sinks from their buildings as early as 1902, but most owners deferred removal until at least 1904.[56] On the section of Orchard Street in the Tenth Ward, at least twelve old tenements had their outdoor privies removed in 1904 and removal work began on an additional ten buildings in 1905. Many tenement owners chose to comply with the less expensive alternative provided for in the law; for example, by erecting one-story brick and stone or brick and concrete outhouses in the rear yards, thus prolonging the use of outdoor toilets for several decades.

At 97 Orchard Street, in contrast, two water closets and an adjoining fireproof shaft of steel and terra-cotta block were constructed in 1905 on

Figure 44. Toilet compartment installed in 1905 in the hall of 97 Orchard Street, 2005. Photograph by Andrew S. Dolkart.

each floor in a space that had previously been part of the inner bedrooms of the apartments along the south side of the building. Each of the small compartments had a wooden door with figured-glass panels, a window opening onto the air shaft, a slate floor, a porcelain toilet bowl with wood seat, a wood water tank flushed by a pull chain, and gas lighting (Fig. 44).

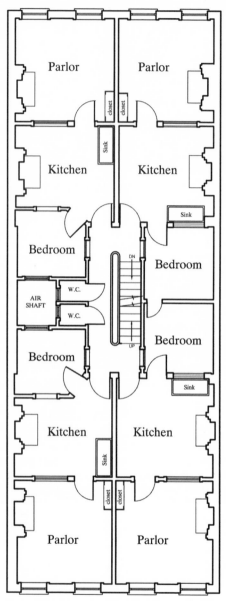

Figure 45. Plan of the upper four floors of 97 Orchard Street in 1905 after the addition of toilets and an air shaft and the rearrangement of all of the walls in the apartments on the south side of the building (left) and the realignment of the kitchen/parlor walls in the northern apartments. Courtesy of Li-Saltzman Architects.

Figure 46. Alberene Stone Company's soapstone washtub (left) added to the apartments at 97 Orchard Street ca. 1905; note the round plaque identifying the Alberene Company just below the rim. To the right is a later porcelain-enamel sink supplied by the Standard Sanitary Manufacturing Company, 2005. Photograph by Andrew S. Dolkart.

The addition of the water closets and the air shaft reduced the square footage of the south apartments from about 350 to 318 square feet and displaced a substantial part of the bedrooms, making these inner rooms uninhabitable. To address this problem and to keep a three-room arrangement in each apartment, the partitions between the kitchen and bedroom in all of the south apartments at 97 Orchard Street were rearranged, reducing the size of the kitchens, but making the bedrooms large enough to be habitable (Fig. 45).[57] Small windows were cut into the new kitchen-bedroom walls and were framed with wood recycled from the surrounds of the previous windows. In addition, a window opening onto the new air shaft was cut into the bedroom wall.

At the same time that the apartments on the south side of the building were so radically reconfigured, changes were also made to the size of the kitchens and parlors in all of the apartments in the building. The walls between these two rooms were moved approximately two feet to enlarge

This is OUR LEADER

Two
Part

Four
Foot

PLATE 103.

Alberene Stone

Laundry Tub with Brass Plugs and Painted Iron Legs.

Price $16.00 as shown.

Figure 47. "Our Leader," soapstone washtub with galvanized-iron legs advertised in an 1899–1900 catalogue of the Alberene Stone Company. Catalogue of the Alberene Stone Company (1899–1900). Courtesy of Avery Architectural and Fine Arts Library, Columbia University in the City of New York.

the size of the kitchens, probably as a result of the addition of water to each apartment.[58] These alterations to the room layouts were planned by architect Otto Reissmann, who also designed the storefronts and undertook other changes to the building in 1905. Little is known about the German-born Reissmann except that he established his office in about 1897 on the Lower East Side and continued in practice until at least 1930.[59] He was one of a number of architects with offices in the neighborhood who specialized in tenement work. Of the forty-four buildings on Orchard Street for which water closet documentation has been found, ten were altered by Reissmann between 1904 and 1908.

Although there is no documentation recording the exact date water was provided to the tenement apartments at 97 Orchard Street, physical evidence (including the similarity between the pipes for the toilets and those for the sinks) combined with limited documentation suggests that this occurred in 1905 at the same time that the toilets were added.[60] By 1905 most tenements already had some form of indoor plumbing, since in 1887 the New York State Legislature mandated the provision of water in all tenements erected after May 14, 1867.[61] The law only required that a building owner install a water line with one sink on each floor. The law did not actually go into effect until 1895 when the New York State Court of Appeals upheld its legality against a challenge by Trinity Church, owner of a great deal of land occupied by old and substandard tenements and converted row houses.[62] In practice, many tenement owners simply added a single water line to their buildings with a common faucet located in the hall on each floor. The New York City Health Department was also empowered to order the installation of water in older tenements, although there is no evidence of such an order for 97 Orchard Street.

As with most alterations in tenement buildings, the installation of cast-iron water pipes, waste pipes, and stone sinks was done in the least expensive way, with the location of the pipes varying in different lines of apartments. At 97 Orchard Street, the water pipes that were apparently installed in 1905 were connected to the existing sewer line that ran through the north side of the cellar. Thus, pipes for the northern apartments—a one-inch cold water pipe, a three-inch waste pipe, and a two-inch vent pipe—were located above the north wall of the kitchens in the apartments on the north side of the tenement.[63] The sinks in these units were located in the northeast corner of the kitchen, beneath the window on the wall separating the kitchen and bedroom. Branch pipes brought water to the south apartments. The length of the branch pipe was kept to a minimum by placing the sinks in these apartments on the north wall of the kitchen, between the apartment's entrance and the entry into the parlor.[64]

The new pipes connected to soapstone tub sinks supplied by the Alberene Stone Company, a firm that was established in 1893 in Virginia. This company supplied gray soapstone fixtures with galvanized iron legs that were referred to in the firm's catalogues as "laundry tubs" (Figs. 46 and 47). According to an 1899–1900 catalogue, they were the company's cheapest fixture, listed at $16.00 each. The tubs were the company's best-seller and were referred to as "Our Leader."[65] These four-foot-long sinks were divided into two basins. Each sink was provided with a bronze cold-water faucet. These sinks served many purposes, providing fresh water, a location for washing dishes and laundering clothing, and even a place for bathing children. Max

Mason, who moved into 97 Orchard Street upon his arrival in New York from Russia in 1921, recalled that "a concrete ["concrete" refers to soapstone] kitchen tub served double duty as a bathing facility and, when covered over with a porcelain tin cover it became a preparation table for mother's cooking needs."[66]

No records specifically confirm when the soapstone sinks were installed. There is some evidence that these sinks were installed in the kitchens, beneath the kitchen/bedroom windows, in the 1890s.[67] There is no evidence that they had a water source, so residents would have had to carry water up to their apartments from the pump in the yard. There may have been wastewater lines connected to the sewer system.

At the same time that the water closets and plumbing were introduced at 97 Orchard Street, the front apartments on the first floor were converted into stores.[68] Architect Otto Reissmann planned the removal of the front wall on the first floor and the construction of wood and cast-iron storefronts resting on the cast-iron piers of the earlier shop fronts at the basement level. These storefronts were painted with a light yellowish-brown lead-based paint and then coated with a brown varnish, crudely creating the appearance of grained golden oak.[69] As part of this alteration project, Reissmann also replaced the original stone stoop with cast-iron steps, new newel posts, and ornate wrought-iron railings (see Fig. 52). The addition of these new storefronts at 97 Orchard Street and on other Lower East Side tenements in the early twentieth century reflects how profitable commercial rentals were to the owners of these buildings.

In 1901, the state legislature established the new Tenement House Department, which was to begin its work on January 1, 1902. The city's new reform mayor, former Columbia University president Seth Low, appointed the department's first commissioner. Although Low was a reformer, he was wary of appointing a commissioner who, like Lawrence Veiller, might be perceived as being too radical. Low finally appointed Robert DeForest commissioner, with Veiller serving as his first deputy. In fact, DeForest was primarily a figurehead, with Veiller functioning as the leading force behind the new department's efforts at improving tenement conditions.[70]

Before it could begin its work, the department hired a staff of inspectors to document the prevailing housing conditions in New York and to make sure that tenement owners were following the requirements of the 1901 law. The department hired both men and women (Figs. 48 and 49), providing each with a uniform and identification badge (Fig. 50). Hiring women as inspectors was a radical idea in 1902, but this innovation was justified, since

Figure 48. Male Tenement House Department inspector, ca. 1903. *First Report of the Tenement House Department of the City of New York,* vol. 1 (1903). Courtesy of Andrew S. Dolkart.

Figure 49. Female Tenement House Department inspector, ca. 1903. *First Report of the Tenement House Department of the City of New York,* vol. 1 (1903). Courtesy of Andrew S. Dolkart.

Figure 50. Badge carried by all Tenement House Department inspectors, ca. 1903. *First Report of the Tenement House Department of the City of New York,* vol. 1 (1903). Courtesy of Andrew S. Dolkart.

women had been deeply involved in the efforts to improve housing in settlement work and in other reform efforts. Inspector Mary Sayles reported the shock of one woman living in a tenement when Sayles explained that she inspected dark cellars and climbed onto roofs: "I never should have dreamed of a female reduced to do such work!"[71]

The new inspectors, however, knew very little about collecting data. They were "totally untrained," according to the anonymous authors of the *First Report of the Tenement House Department*, with no experience "in the practical details of the construction of tenement houses."[72] Thus, the inspectors were carefully trained in survey techniques and were provided with a printed card known as an "I-card" ("I" for "Improvements"). The card provided categories and questions that guided the inspector in recording conditions. The card was arranged so that it would be completed in the order of the inspector's visit, starting with the roof and descending to the cellar. The inspector would note conditions of the roof, skylight, shafts, windows, fire escapes, sinks, toilets, interior rooms, and so on, and was also asked to draw a plan of the building, measuring the size of each room.[73] Between May 28, 1902 and February 9, 1903, every tenement in New York City was examined by a departmental inspector. The I-card for 97 Orchard Street was completed on October 7, 1902. The inspector recorded twenty-two apartments, including two in the basement. He also noted the presence of six school sinks on the south side of the rear yard, but the museum's 1991–93 archaeological investigation uncovered no evidence of toilets in this location, indicating that the inspectors were not always diligent about completing the I-cards correctly.[74] However, the inspector did find several conditions that did not meet the requirements of the new tenement law, including an inadequate skylight over the stairwell, and a cellar that was not watertight.

The 1901 Tenement House Act and its amendments and the law that created the Tenement House Department did not create ideal housing for New York's poorest residents. Rather, the law improved the quality of new housing and forced owners to institute modest improvements in older buildings. The Tenement House Committee of the Charity Organization Society, which had initially proposed the reform law, issued another report in 1914 that reviewed changes since 1901. The report found "the worst conditions in the older tenements have been done away with. Over 7,000 vile privies in the crowded, closely built-up sections of the city, each a dangerous centre of disease, have been completely removed, and new, modern, sanitary conveniences installed instead. The tuberculosis-breeding inside dark room is rapidly becoming a thing of the past. Over 200,000 rooms previously without any windows whatsoever, mere dark closets, have had windows cut into them letting in a little of the outside light and air."[75]

6

THE CHANGING CHARACTER
OF THE LOWER EAST SIDE
IN THE EARLY TWENTIETH CENTURY

The Tenement House Department's 1902–03 survey not only detailed conditions in every individual tenement in New York, but also provided the data for a comprehensive analysis of tenement conditions in the city. This analysis of housing conditions was the first since the Council of Hygiene and Public Health's study in 1864. It documented the total number of tenements and their physical characteristics, detailed the size and population density of every tenement block, and provided information on the number, size, and nationality of a tenement's residents.[1]

The survey found that in 1903 the Tenth Ward—bounded by the Bowery on the west, Norfolk Street on the east, Rivington Street on the north, and Division Street on the south—was the most densely populated ward in the city, with a population of 69,944 or approximately 665 people per acre. The most densely populated block in the ward was number 414, the block on which 97 Orchard Street is located (the survey was completed before the size of the block was reduced; see Fig. 53). This block covered 2.04 acres and had a total population of 2,223 people (1,089 people per acre), comprising 450 families. They resided in thirty-four buildings: two surviving two-and-one-half-story row houses, twenty-eight pre-law tenements (such as 97 Orchard Street), and four dumbbell tenements.[2] The vast majority of residents were from

PRICE, 15c.

AND UP

97 Orchard Street,

Bet. Delancy & Broome Sts.   1st Fl. Back, Room 4, N. Y.

The World Famous Palmist and Mind Reader recently arrived from Europe.

PROF. DORA MELTZER,

She guesses the name and age of Every Person. She is an unexcelled Palmist, tells you the past, present and future, gives the best advice in business, journeys, Law Suits, Love, Sickness, Family affairs, etc.

Open from 9 A. M. to 10 P. M.

97 Orchard Street,

Bet. Delancy & Broome Sts.   1st Fl. Back, Room 4, N.

Figure 51. Handbill for "world famous" Dora Meltzer, who read palms and minds from the apartment at 97 Orchard Street where she lived with her brother's family. Courtesy of Lower East Side Tenement Museum.

Russia (undoubtedly Russian Jews). Of the 310 heads of families, 186 were of Russian parentage; the next largest groups were from Austria-Hungary (52) and Germany (29).[3] Statistics for the entire ward were similar. Of the 13,544 heads of families, 8,369 were of Russian parentage.[4] The families living in the block's small apartments were large; of the 310 tenement households, 176 had five or more members.[5] 97 Orchard Street reflected the ethnic make-up of the neighborhood. Of the 111 residents recorded in the 1900 census, sixty-two were born in Russia, with an additional nineteen children born in the United States to Russian immigrant parents.

The increasing number of residents at 97 Orchard Street, which peaked at 111 in 1900, also reflects the increasing population density throughout the Lower East Side. In 1870, seventy-two people were recorded as living in the new tenement at 97 Orchard Street. This number rose slightly, to eighty people in 1880 and then to ninety-six in 1890, and 111 in 1900. By 1910, the population had declined slightly to 101.[6] It is during the late nineteenth century and first years of the twentieth century, when the population was highest, that factories operated in the building. Other tenants also appear to have worked out of their apartments. "The World Famous Palmist and Mind Reader" Dora Meltzer, "recently arrived from Europe," told the "past, present and future" and offered advice on business, love, and other matters from an apartment at 97 Orchard Street (Fig. 51).[7]

Typifying the Russian Jewish immigrant families that settled in the Tenth Ward were the Rogarshevskys, a family of eight who moved into 97 Orchard Street some time between 1906 and 1910 and remained in the building until the 1930s (Fig. 52). In 1901, Abram and Zipe Heller and their five children left Telsh (or Telz), Lithuania, a part of the Russian empire, for New York. On the trip, they Americanized their first names to Abraham and Fannie and changed their last name to Rogarshevsky, the name of their American sponsor (in about 1925, the family name was changed again, to Rosenthal). After arriving in America, one daughter died, but two sons were born.

Like many Jewish immigrants, Abraham Rogarshevsky worked in the garment industry, as a presser. Two of the Rogarshevsky daughters also worked in garment factories. In 1918, Abraham Rogarshevsky died of tuberculosis, one of the deadliest diseases in New York in the early years of the twentieth century. With her husband dead, Fannie Rogarshevsky needed a job and soon became the janitor of 97 Orchard Street, working for the building's owner, Russian Jewish immigrant Moishe Helpern. Even after the apartments at 97 Orchard Street were vacated and the building ceased to be

Figure 52. Members of the Rogarshevsky family standing in front of the stoop at 97 Orchard Street, ca. 1915. Courtesy of Lower East Side Tenement Museum.

a residential structure in 1935, Fannie stayed on as janitor. Fannie and Abraham were Orthodox and closely followed the Sabbath prohibition against work between sundown on Friday and sundown on Saturday. Thus their non-Jewish neighbor, Josephine Baldizzi, switched their apartment lights on and off for them on the Sabbath: I can still see Mrs. Rosenthal in the air shaft window, waving to me, motioning for me to come in and to turn on the lights because it was the Sabbath, the Jewish holiday, and they weren't allowed to touch the electricity. And it made me very proud to have to do that.[8] The extraordinary population density in the Tenth Ward and neighboring Lower East Side wards in the early twentieth century was caused by several factors. The major cause was the increasing population of immigrants, mostly Eastern European Jews and Italians, who arrived in New York City during that period. Many of these immigrants initially settled on the Lower East Side, Jews largely east of the Bowery and Italians largely to the west, because it was an area with affordable housing marketed to immigrants. In addition, particular ethnic or religious groups tended to settle where others from their groups had already established themselves and thus could ease their transition to life in America.

Overcrowding was also aggravated by developments in specific neigh-

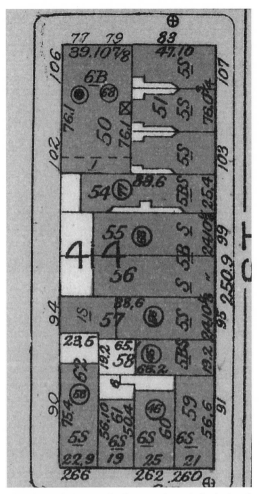

Figure 53. Map of block on which 97 Orchard Street is located after both Delancey and Allen Streets had been widened, 1934. G. W. Bromley & Company, *Manhattan Land Book* (1934). Courtesy of Andrew S. Dolkart.

borhoods, some of which were the unintended by-products of government projects supported by the progressive reformers. For example, the demolition of blocks of tenements for the construction of schools, parks, and other structures resulted in the displacement of large numbers of people and their relocation into already overcrowded tenements. Reformers, for example, had campaigned for the construction of small parks and playgrounds in the city's overcrowded immigrant neighborhoods. The construction of Seward

Park and Hamilton Fish Park in the primarily Jewish area of the Lower East Side in the late 1890s brought much needed recreational space to the neighborhood, but resulted in the demolition of entire blocks of tenements and the displacement of more than 6,000 people.[9] The widening of Delancey Street in the first years of the twentieth century to create a boulevard leading onto the Williamsburg Bridge also required the demolition of numerous buildings and displaced thousands of people, including many living in buildings on the north half of the block on which 97 Orchard Street is located. The size of this block was further truncated in 1931–32 when Allen Street was widened by removing the entire western half of the block (Fig. 53); as a result, more light was provided to the rear apartments at 97 Orchard Street.[10]

Although no statistical information is available, anecdotal evidence suggests that most of the Jewish residents displaced by these projects (especially in the late nineteenth century and first years of the twentieth century) remained on the Lower East Side close to friends, family, and a community that spoke Yiddish, shared social and religious customs, and provided synagogues, kosher food stores, and other community facilities. In a report on the effect of displacement due to the demolition of buildings on Delancey Street, the *Real Estate Record* noted, in somewhat derogatory terms, that "nearly all the tenants of the demolished buildings were Hebrews, whose friends and associates live in the vicinity. This class of Hebrews is extremely clannish, and although some of the real estate agents made attempts to get them to move into the cheaper tenement sections uptown, their efforts were futile. Several families moved in May up around 42d st. and they are now either back in the district or are seeking quarters there."[11] The neighborhood was also within convenient walking distance to the new loft buildings where many immigrants were employed in garment factories. Had they moved to neighborhoods uptown or in other boroughs, they would have had to commute on the elevated railroads—or, after October 1904, on the subway—spending a precious nickel for the fare in each direction.

During the early decades of the twentieth century two notable utilities were upgraded in the apartments at 97 Orchard Street. At an unknown date, additional water lines were installed and a second sink was added in the kitchen of each apartment, providing, for the first time, both hot and cold water. An inexpensive iron sink with porcelain-enamel finish was hung from the kitchen wall on a metal bracket (see Fig. 46). These sinks were the least expensive unit manufactured by the Standard Sanitary Manufacturing Company of Pittsburgh, a major supplier of kitchen and

Patented July 13, 1909
Patented August 10, 1909

Plate P 6800 D

Figure 54. Iron roll-rim sink with porcelain-enamel finish, of the type installed in the apartments at 97 Orchard Street, illustrated in a 1911 catalogue of the Standard Sanitary Manufacturing Company. *Standard Bathroom and Plumbing Fixtures Catalogue P* (1911). Courtesy of Avery Architectural and Fine Arts Library, Columbia University in the City of New York.

bathroom fixtures (Fig. 54).[12] Similar changes took place in many of the other old tenements in the city (Fig. 55). In addition, electricity was added to the building at some point after 1918, evidenced by the patent date on the electrical panels located at the rear of the hall on the first floor. One former tenant remembers that electricity was added in 1924, the year he entered kindergarten.[13] Even after electric lighting had been installed, Josephine Baldizzi remembers that in the 1930s the lighting was "very dull, very dim."[14]

In the second and third decades of the twentieth century, the population at 97 Orchard Street and in other Lower East Side tenements became more diverse as the Eastern European Jews who had dominated the area for several decades were joined by Jews from the former Ottoman Empire. The 1915 New York State census records a predominance of Russian immigrants, including six members of the Rogarshevsky family, but also records three households from Turkey.[15] Among these were the ten members of the Confino family (Fig. 56). The Confinos had lived a middle-class life in Kas-

Figure 55. Tenement kitchen at 263 Stanton Street in 1923, with many features similar to those at 97 Orchard Street, including stone washtub, porcelain-enamel sink, interior window, wooden cupboard, and linoleum floor. Courtesy of The Irma and Paul Milstein Division of United States, Local History and Genealogy (New York City Street Views), The New York Public Library, Astor Lenox and Tilden Foundations.

toria, Turkey (now part of Greece), running a grocery store, but in about 1913, after Abraham Confino's store burned down, he, his wife Rachel, and their four sons and one daughter left for New York where an older daughter and her husband already lived. This family of seven moved into a cramped fifth-floor apartment at 97 Orchard Street. The size of the household further increased with the birth of another daughter and, by 1915, the presence of two nephews. Abraham Confino initially supported his family by selling goods from a pushcart before opening his own underwear factory on Allen Street. As with most immigrants, the Confinos struggled with issues of tradition and assimilation: sons Jacob, Salvatore, and Saul Americanized their first names to Jack, Charlie, and Bob, and son David persuaded most members of the family to change their surname to Coffield. The Confino family moved out of 97 Orchard Street in 1917, relocating to East Harlem, the neighborhood in Manhattan with the second-largest immigrant Jewish community.[16]

The 1920 US census records five apartments at 97 Orchard Street hous-

Figure 56. Confino family, ca. 1911. Courtesy of Lower East Side Tenement Museum.

ing Sephardic Jews from Turkey and Greece and records that their "mother tongue" was Spanish. Sephardic Jews trace their ancestry to the Jews expelled from Spain in 1492. Sephardic communities, especially those in the Ottoman Empire, continued to speak a fifteenth-century Spanish, with the addition of some words from Turkish, Arabic, Greek, Hebrew, and other languages. This Judeo-Spanish language, known as Ladino, was generally written in Hebrew script and retains many archaic words that are no longer part of modern Spanish.[17]

At least one Jewish household from the former Ottoman Empire, that of Morris and Beckie Abrams, was not Sephardic. The Abrams were Romaniote Jews, a small group of Greek-speakers from what is now northern Greece. The group's ancestors had lived in Greece from the first century and had developed its own customs and rituals, which differed from those of the more dominant Ashkenazic and Sephardic communities.[18] Morris Abrams came to New York from Janina, Greece, in 1909, while Beckie Elias arrived in 1912. Morris and Beckie married in 1919 and moved into a top-floor front apartment at 97 Orchard Street with Morris's widowed mother Sophie. Morris's sister Rebecca and her husband Max Eskinazi, also from Janina, soon moved into another apartment on the same floor. Beckie gave birth to four children (one of whom died of the measles and pneumonia) in the apartment before the family moved into a tenement on East 114th Street in Harlem in 1927.[19]

In addition to the influx of Jews from what are now Turkey and Greece, Italian immigrants began moving into the area from Little Italy—west of the Bowery—in the late 1920s. In 1928, Sicilian immigrants Adolfo and Rosaria Baldizzi, their two-year-old daughter Josephine, and their baby son John (Fig. 57) moved from Elizabeth Street in the heart of the Italian Lower East Side into one of the small apartments on the south side of 97 Orchard Street. Adolfo had been in New York since 1923, when he had arrived as an illegal stowaway. The Baldizzi family owned very little, and, according to Josephine, the apartment was sparsely furnished. Although Adolfo was a trained cabinetmaker work was difficult to find, especially during the Depression when he was forced to become an itinerant handyman, carrying his toolbox in search of odd jobs. When the owner of 97 Orchard Street decided to close the residential floors of the building in 1935, the Baldizzis were evicted and moved to nearby Eldridge Street.[20]

Several trends caused the owner of 97 Orchard Street to stop renting apartments in 1935. By 1930, the Lower East Side had lost a significant part of its population, and vacancy rates had climbed in the neighborhood's tenements. This is evidenced by the fact that, in 1925, only fifty-six people lived at 97 Orchard Street and almost half of the apartments were empty.[21] The declining population was partly due to the passage of a restrictive, racially motivated immigration law in 1924 that specifically sought to slow the immigration of Jews, Italians, and other Eastern and Southern Europeans. The Johnson-Reed

Figure 57. Josephine Baldizzi and her brother John on the roof of 97 Orchard Street, ca. 1934. Courtesy of Lower East Side Tenement Museum.

Act established national quotas, limiting immigration from every European country to two percent of its total US population in 1890, before large-scale migration from Eastern and Southern Europe had begun. As a result, this law significantly limited the number of new immigrant residents to the neighborhood. This reduction in the number of new immigrants settling on the Lower East Side was coupled with the fact that as the garment trade became increasingly unionized and wages rose, older immigrants prospered.

With new subway lines extending into the outer regions of the city,

Figure 58. The Brandies & Marcus General Merchandise auction house, ca. 1938, in the south storefront at 97 Orchard Street; Herman Brandies is standing at left; Max Marcus is standing at right, with his brother-in-law, Frank Bloom, in the center. Courtesy of Library of Congress.

many left the Lower East Side, relocating to less densely populated neighborhoods in Brooklyn, the Bronx, and Queens where more modern, technologically up-to-date apartments were available at reasonable rents. According to the US census, in the ten years between 1920 and 1930 the population of the Lower East Side declined from 414,909 to 248,696, a loss of 166,213 people. By 1933, the apartment vacancy rate had reached 22.4 percent in the neighborhood.[22] By the 1930s, 97 Orchard Street was one of the oldest surviving tenements on the Lower East Side. This deteriorating building, with its small apartments, dark inner bedrooms, and hall toilets, could not have been competitive even during the Depression, as neighborhood residents sought out better apartments.

With declining rent rolls due to this precipitous decline in population, Moishe Helpern and many other Lower East Side landlords had no financial incentive to spend capital to meet the stringent requirements of a new tenement law passed in May 1934, which required the removal of all wood in the public halls.[23] Helpern would have had to invest in the removal of all of the pine wainscoting and, most significantly, the replacement of the entire wood staircase with a costly stair of metal or some other incombustible material. Instead, he chose to close the four upper floors in mid-1935.[24] On October 11, 1935, an inspector reported that 97 Orchard Street was vacant except for its stores and a caretaker's apartment, inhabited by Fannie Rosenthal.[25]

Helpern was not alone in abandoning residential use of his building. A significant number of tenement apartments on Orchard Street and on other Lower East Side streets were vacated during the 1930s. Indeed, some owners not only stopped renting apartments, but actually demolished the former residential upper floors of their buildings. The tenements were not, however, totally abandoned, since the popularity of Orchard and nearby streets for shopping generated sufficient rents from the stores to assure the survival of most buildings. In fact, with the demolition of the tenements and other buildings on the east side of Allen Street in 1931–32, property values rose on the west side of Orchard Street, since the commercial establishments now had two street fronts.[26] Shops that occupied space in the four stores at 97 Orchard Street during the next several decades included purveyors of hats, handbags, hosiery, and ladies' clothing, and an auction house (Fig. 58). At least one store used the upper floors for storage, as is evident from inventory notes penciled on the walls and woodwork tallying the number of dresses, blouses, skirts, and other items in stock (Fig. 59). 97 Orchard Street remained a viable commercial building for decades, remaining in the hands of the Helpern family. In 1988, however, a new chapter began in the history of this old tenement: its conversion into the Lower East Side Tenement Museum.

Figure 59. Inventory penciled onto a doorjamb in a first-floor apartment at 97 Orchard Street, ca. 2000. Courtesy of Lower East Side Tenement Museum (photograph by Jerome Liebling).

CREATING THE LOWER EAST SIDE TENEMENT MUSEUM

The opening of Washington's Revolutionary War head-quarters in Newburg, New York, and his Virginia home, Mt. Vernon, along the Potomac River near Washington, D.C., in the mid-nineteenth century marked the beginning of Americans' fascination with historic house museums. Almost all of these museums celebrated the lives of historically important figures or were preserved because of their age or architectural significance. The few house museums that celebrate ordinary people include farmhouses and log cabins in rural locations. While most of these are worthy of preservation, none focuses on the lives of the tens of thousands of immigrants who settled in American cities beginning in the 1840s. In 1985, Ruth J. Abram set out to redress this omission by establishing an organization that would focus on the immigrant experience in urban tenements. As Abram noted, "we have preserved log cabins and farm houses and honored the gentry by preserving their mansions in homage to our rural history. But most Americans have their roots in urban America and the tenement is the quintessential embodiment of that experience."[1] In addition, Abram wanted to celebrate all immigrant traditions, comparing experiences, good and bad, of past immigrants with those of the present day, to "create a vibrant beacon for tolerance."[2]

Initially, Abram and curator Anita Jacobson ran a

public history project without a home. In 1988, Jacobson responded to a "for rent" sign at 97 Orchard Street, and this fledgling museum settled into a tenement storefront. This building proved to be the perfect location for the museum, with its upper floors untouched since the owner stopped renting apartments in 1935. After occupying the building for eight years, the Lower East Side Tenement Museum purchased 97 Orchard Street in 1996.

Although the Tenement Museum found its home in 1988, it was not ready to receive visitors. The museum needed a plan to guide the conversion of the building into a museum that would embody the institution's mission. The task of planning the museum was especially complex because the museum's guiding vision was not to restore the building to reflect conditions at one specific time, but to explore the experiences of many different immigrant groups over the entire period of the building's occupancy and to relate these experiences of the past with contemporary immigrant issues. As the museum's initial mission statement put it, its goal has been to "promote tolerance and historical perspective through the presentation and interpretation of the variety of immigrant and migrant experiences in Manhattan's Lower East Side, a gateway to America."[3]

In 1991, with funding from the National Endowment for the Humanities, historians, museum professionals, artists, community representatives, and individuals from other fields assembled to write preliminary reports on issues that could be explored in the museum and to discuss the most effective ways to convert the abandoned apartments into powerful museum exhibitions. At one of these meetings, Kenneth Ames, an historian of material culture, suggested that the museum should reject the idea of fabricating immigrant stories and, rather, tell the stories of the people who had lived in the building. This idea became the basis for subsequent in-depth research into the building's inhabitants. Census enumerations, Civil War draft records, voter lists, school records, birth and death certificates, court records, factory inspector lists, city directories, and many other historic sources were scoured in order to find the names of people who had lived at 97 Orchard Street and to cull information about their lives. These records became the basis for interpreting several of the museum apartments. For example, the apartment of German immigrant Nathalie Gumpertz relies heavily on Surrogate Court records detailing how she had been abandoned by her husband and subsequently established a dressmaking business in her apartment; the lists compiled during the late nineteenth and early twentieth centuries by the New York State Factory Inspector and published in a series of annual reports documented Harris Levine as the proprietor of a

Figure 60. The Levine's tenement factory in 1897 as reconstructed by the Tenement Museum in 2002. Courtesy of Lower East Side Tenement Museum (photograph by Benjamin Trimmier).

small garment factory in the building (Fig. 60). In addition, the museum advertised in newspapers written for specific ethnic and religious readers and in publications such as *Modern Maturity*, seeking people who had lived at 97 Orchard Street. Josephine Baldizzi, Henry Rosenthal, and others who were raised at 97 Orchard Street were interviewed, and their stories were incorporated into presentations of their tenement apartments. Thus, one can visit the Baldizzi apartment on the day they were moving out of the building in 1935 and the Rogarshevsky (Rosenthal) apartment in 1915 as Fannie Rogarshevsky is preparing the apartment for Sabbath dinner. These historical records and interviews were the start of efforts to interpret the museum apartments, with urban historians, architects, architectural historians, museum designers, preservationists, genealogists, archaeologists, material culture specialists, folklorists, ethnic historians, engineers, photographers, conservators, archivists, and others contributing their expertise to each aspect of the interpretation and restoration of the building.

Just as important as the interpretation of the individual apartments and their inhabitants was the interpretation of the building itself. Indeed, the building was both the most important artifact in the museum's collection and the major obstacle to the institution's success. The tenement not only had serious structural problems that needed to be addressed, but even more problematic was the fact that public entry to the upper floors of the building did not meet contemporary fire and safety codes—there was no functional secondary means of egress, halls were exceptionally narrow, and the public areas were constructed of combustible materials. It was also imperative that a strategy be devised to protect the layers of physical history evident within the building, since one of the aspects that makes this building such a powerful historical statement is the clear evidence of successive residents and alterations, with layers of paint and wallpaper, peeling plaster, bulging walls, abandoned sinks, and other features providing evidence of the lives of the thousands who moved through this structure and similar buildings across the city (Fig. 61).

In order to solve the problems relating to stabilization, restoration, and public access, the Tenement Museum hired Li-Saltzman Architects, a small architectural firm headed by Roz Li and Judith Saltzman that specializes in historic preservation issues. The firm immediately began work on structural and code issues. Li-Saltzman then began working with the museum's expanding professional staff, establishing the preservation philosophy that has guided all of the work on the building and on the creation of the museum apartments. Saltzman has summarized the philosophy behind the preservation of the building:

> The preservation of 97 Orchard Street is predicated on retaining the palpable sense of history contained within its walls, and on providing both the experience of the tenement as people lived there, and as it was found. To do so, it is critical to identify appropriate ways of treating the building's historic fabric. The philosophy for the treatment of 97 Orchard Street is based on several key goals: to provide safe

Figure 61. An unrestored apartment at 97 Orchard Street. Courtesy of Lower East Side Tenement Museum.

> public access to the historic resource; to respect the contributions of all periods of the site's historic significance (1863–1935); to maximize the retention of the site's historic character; to minimize the loss of extant historic fabric; [and] to integrate historic preservation with the interpretive program.[4]

The first issues addressed involved safety. Working closely with the city's Department of Buildings, the museum and its architects developed ways to insure safety while maintaining the building's historic fabric, notably the woodwork in the halls and apartments. Since all of the buildings on the east side of Allen Street were demolished in the 1930s, the museum was able to build a fire stair on the rear facade, leading directly to the street. In addition, sprinklers were installed in all interior spaces and a code-compliant fire escape, adapting the design of the original fire escape, was constructed in the front of the building. The need to install sprinklers (and heaters to keep them from freezing), self-closing door hinges, emergency lighting, and other modern fixtures to meet code requirements introduced an important philosophical preservation issue: Should these new additions be as unobtrusive as possible, as they are in most house museums, or should they be visible? As noted above, a key goal of the Tenement Museum is to preserve the surviving evidence of decades of alterations to the building in response to the changing needs of the tenants and to the requirements of tenement

Figure 62. The Rogarshevsky apartment as reconstructed by the Tenement Museum in 1998. Courtesy of Lower East Side Tenement Museum.

reform laws. At 97 Orchard Street additions such as the toilets, air shaft, gas fixtures, water pipes, sinks, and interior windows are all clearly visible. Thus, it was decided that all new additions to meet contemporary code requirements should be just as visible as are the earlier changes.

In order to preserve the interior fabric of the building and, at the same time, restore apartments to reflect particular periods in the building's history, the museum decided that two of the four apartments on each floor would be stabilized and preserved as they were found when the museum took ownership, and that the eight remaining apartments would be restored. In fact, on most tours through the museum, the first apartment that a visitor enters is preserved in its vacant, deteriorated condition. Visitors are therefore able to stand in the small, unfurnished space and reflect on their own family histories and their own connections or reactions to tenement life. In addition, the halls and toilets remain as they were found. Since 1994, when the first apartments were opened to the public, five historic apartments have been created (Fig. 62) and a sixth has been reconstructed in a former store space.[5]

The museum staff and its architects also needed to decide how the exterior would be restored. The facade had been altered in 1905, with the addition of storefronts on the first story and the replacement of the original stone entrance stoop with an iron stoop; thus 1905 was chosen as the date for exterior restoration. Unfortunately, the storefronts were badly deteriorated, and the iron stoop had been replaced in the 1940s. However, detailed analysis of the surviving sections of the storefronts made possible their physical restoration and the recreation of the original crude-grained finish. The character of the stoop was also documented in a small family snapshot from around 1915, of the Rogarshevsky family standing in front of the building (see Fig. 52). Fortuitously, the family had posed just to the right of the stoop's handrail, permitting a clear view of the stairs and railing. Li-Saltzman digitally enhanced elements of the stoop and then searched for similar examples still extant on nearby buildings. This work resulted in the restoration of the lower facade so that it now closely resembles that installed by Otto Reissman in 1905 (Fig. 63).

Work on the Tenement Museum's building at 97 Orchard Street is a continuing process. Investigations continue on the history of the physical fabric in order to solve mysteries about the specific features of the building. New findings have changed the interpretation of the building and its residents in small and large ways and other changes have occurred as additional spaces have opened for visitation and as the museum's staff develops programs to improve the experience of visitors.[6] The museum has been extraordinarily successful, perhaps even beyond the initial vision of Ruth Abram. The importance of this pioneering institution has been widely recognized. In 1992, 97 Orchard Street was listed on the National Register of Historic Places. Two years later, the building was designated a National Historic Landmark, joining the Statue of Liberty, Independence Hall, and Mt. Vernon on the list of America's most distinguished historic sites (the National Park Service has designated fewer than 2,500 National Historic Landmarks). In 1998, the museum officially became the Lower East Side Tenement National Historic Site and Affiliated Area of the National Park Service. The popularity of the museum—which received almost 175,000 visitors during the 2011 fiscal year—demonstrates how much interest there is among Americans in the everyday history of the nation and its people. In addition, the various historic designations reflect how the historic preservation movement and the study of American history have expanded and matured in recent years to include recognition of the significance and contributions of ordinary people and vernacular buildings in the creation of America.

Figure 63. Storefront of 97 Orchard Street as restored by Li-Saltzman Architects in 2004. Courtesy of Lower East Side Tenement Museum (photograph by Greg Scaffidi).

NOTES

INTRODUCTION

1.   Lawrence Veiller, "Tenement House Reform in New York City, 1834–1900," in Robert W. DeForest and Lawrence Veiller, eds., *The Tenement House Problem*, vol. 1 (New York: Macmillan, 1903), 69–118; James Ford, *Slums and Housing* (Cambridge, Mass.: Harvard University Press, 1936); Roy Lubove, *The Progressives and the Slums: Tenement House Reform in New York City 1890–1917* (Pittsburgh: University of Pittsburgh Press, 1962); Anthony Jackson, *A Place Called Home: A History of Low-Cost Housing in Manhattan* (Cambridge, Mass.: MIT Press, 1976); Richard Plunz, *A History of Housing in New York City: Dwelling Type and Social Change in the American Metropolis* (New York: Columbia University Press, 1990).

2.   The paucity of studies on individual tenement buildings parallels the findings of urban historian Dolores Hayden regarding post–World War II suburbs: "Although many sociologists found it fascinating to interview suburbanites about issues of social conformity, surprisingly few detailed studies were made of the built environment of large, postwar suburbs. These places have not attracted architectural historians, because few well-known architects were involved, or planning historians, because they were not usually planned by noted practitioners." Dolores Hayden, *Building Suburbia: Green Fields and Urban Growth, 1820–2000* (New York: Pantheon Books, 2000), 128.

EARLY DEVELOPMENT
ON THE LOWER EAST SIDE

1.   The De Lancey grid is evident on "Plan of the City of New York, in North America" [The Ratzer Map] (1777), in I. N. Phelps Stokes, *Iconography of Manhattan Island 1498-1909*, vol. 1 (New York: Robert H. Dodd, 1915), plate 41. Stokes, *iconography*, vol. 5 (1926), 1095, 1193; vol. 6 (1928), 86-87.

2.   Stokes, *Iconography*, vol. 5 (1926), 1095; vol 6. (1928), 86–94.

3.   Elizabeth Blackmar, *Manhattan For Rent, 1785–1850* (Ithaca: Cornell University Press, 1989), 103; this book provides a comprehensive analysis of real estate development in the era before widespread tenement construction. Stokes, *Iconography*, vol. 4 (1922), 752, notes that on October 31, 1765, "Hendrick Rutgers and James Delancey entered into an agreement 'for the settling & establishing of partition Lines between their respective Lands in the Out Ward & for opening & establishing a public Street or Highway' between their lands." This "Street or Highway" became Division Street.

4.   Joan H. Geismar, "The 97 Orchard Street Block and Lot—An Archaeological Perspective," unpublished manuscript, 1991 (Tenement Museum Archives, New York City), 5–6.

5.   Marc A. Weiss, "John Jacob Astor," in Kenneth T. Jackson, ed., *Encyclopedia of New York City* 2nd edition (New Haven: Yale University Press, 2010), 72; Kenneth Wiggins Porter, *John Jacob Astor, Business Man* (Cambridge, Mass.: Harvard University Press, 1931); and Axel Madsen, *John Jacob Astor: America's First Multimillionaire* (New York: John Wiley & Sons, 2001).

6.   Almost all of the churches erected on the Lower East Side during the first half of the nineteenth century were Protestant, reflecting the denominational affiliation of most of the people who were settling in the area's new houses. A number of these early Protestant churches are extant, although they are not owned by their original congregations. Among the more prominent survivors are the Willett Street Methodist Episcopal Church (now the Bialystoker Synagogue; 1826) on Bialystoker Place (formerly Willett Street); the Norfolk Street Baptist Church (now Beth Hamedrash Hagodol Synagogue; 1850) on Norfolk Street; All Saints' Free Episcopal Church (now St. Augustine's Episcopal Church; 1849) on Henry Street; and the Rutgers Presbyterian Church (now St. Teresa's Roman Catholic Church; 1841) on Rutgers Street.

7. Jonathan Greenleaf, *A History of the Churches of All Denominations in the City of New York City, From the First Settlement to the Year 1846* (New York: E. French, 1846), 44, 348.

8. City directories record the presence of the Universalist Church in 1832. Greenleaf, *A History of the Churches*, 348, incorrectly notes that the church was purchased by the Universalists in 1832; see Geismar, "The 97 Orchard Street Block and Lot," 7. Two windows installed by the Universalists were removed and are now in the church of the Second Universalist Society of Stamford, Connecticut. The windows are thought to be Italian, dating from the sixteenth or seventeenth century. For information on these windows, discovered by Tenement Museum intern Andy Urban, see *A Story of One Hundred Years: 1841–1941, Of the Second Universalist Society of Stamford, Connecticut* (1941).

9. Stanley Nadel, *Little Germany: Ethnicity, Religion, and Class in New York City, 1845–80* (Chicago: University of Chicago Press, 1990), 92, notes that Roman Catholics were the largest denomination in *Kleindeutschland*, with only small numbers of Protestant worshipers.

10. For a discussion of the development of new neighborhoods in the nineteenth century, see Charles Lockwood, *Bricks and Brownstone: The New York Row House, 1783–1929, An Architectural and Social History* (New York: McGraw-Hill, 1972; reprinted, New York: Rizzoli, 2003); and Charles Lockwood, *Manhattan Moves Uptown: An Illustrated History* (Boston: Houghton Mifflin, 1976).

11. For population figures, see Ira Rosenwaike, *Population History of New York City* (Syracuse: Syracuse University Press, 1972), 36.

12. New York City Department of Finance, Conveyance Records, block 414 lots 53–55.

13. New York City Department of Finance, Assessed Valuation of Real Estate, 1864.

14. New York City Death Records (1863), New York City Department of Records, Municipal Archives

THE TENEMENT AND ITS INHABITANTS

1. *Laws of New York*, Chapter 908, Section 17 (1867).

2. *Laws of New York*, Chapter 85, Section 13 (1887).

3. Elizabeth Collins Cromley, *Alone Together: A History of New York's Early Apartments* (Ithaca: Cornell University Press), 1990, 5–6, 62.

4.   New York City Department of Buildings, "Communications from the Superintendent of Buildings, Transmitting His Semi-Annual Report for the Half Year Ending December 31st, 1862," 12.

5.   Edward K. Spann, "The Greatest Grid: The New York Plan of 1811," in Daniel Schaffer, ed., *Two Centuries of American Planning* (Baltimore: Johns Hopkins University Press, 1988), 14.

6.   Ernest Flagg, "The New York Tenement-House Evil and its Cure," *Scribner's* 16 (July 1894): 109.

7.   The origins of the first tenement are discussed in James Ford, *Slums and Housing* (Cambridge, Mass.: Harvard University Press, 1936), 95; Edward Lubitz, "The Tenement Problem in New York City and the Movement for its Reform 1856–1867" (PhD diss., New York University, 1970), 4; Elizabeth Blackmar, *Manhattan For Rent, 1785–1950* (Ithaca: Cornell University Press, 1989), 200–01; and Richard Plunz, *A History of Housing in New York City: Dwelling Type and Social Change in the American Metropolis* (New York: Columbia University Press, 1990), 6.

8.   Blackmar, *Manhattan For Rent*, 206–07; Robert A. M. Stern, Thomas Mellins, and David Fishman, *New York 1880: Architecture and Urbanism in the Gilded Age* (New York: Monacelli Press, 1999), 498.

9.   Dr. Griscom's concerns, especially as stated in his pamphlet "A Brief View of the Sanitary Conditions of the City" (1842), are discussed in detail in Lawrence Veiller, "Tenement House Reform in New York City, 1834–1900," in Robert E. DeForest and Lawrence Veiller, eds., *The Tenement House Problem*, vol. 1 (New York: Macmillan, 1903), 71–75; and in Plunz, *A History of Housing*, 4–5.

10.   Veiller, "Tenement House Reform in New York City," 76. The importance of the AICP is also discussed in Roy Lubove, *The Progressives and the Slums: Tenement House Reform in New York City 1890–1917* (Pittsburgh: University of Pittsburgh Press, 1962), 4–11.

11.   Veiller, "Tenement House Reform in New York City," 76.

12.   The Workingmen's Home, now demolished, contained eighty-seven apartments of three rooms each plus a large clothes closet. The staircases were fireproof and the halls were lighted by gas. Each family had its own toilet in the yard. The Workingmen's Home is discussed in Veiller, "Tenement House Reform in New York City," 85–87; Plunz, *A History of Housing*, 7–8; and Robert A. M. Stern, Thomas Mellins, and David Fishman, *New York 1880: Architecture and Urbanism in the Gilded Age* (New York: Monacelli Press, 1999), 502–03.

13.   For A. T. White's projects see Veiller, "Tenement House Reform

in New York City," 97–99; Plunz, *A History of Housing*, 89–93; James Ford, *Slums and Housing* (Cambridge, Mass.: Harvard University Press, 1936), 160–161; Olive and Ari Hoogenboom, "Alfred T. White: Settlement Worker and Housing Reformer," *Hayes Historical Journal* 9 (Fall 1989): 5–31; Alfred T. White, *Better Homes for Workingmen* (New York: Putnam, 1885), *Improved Dwellings for the Laboring Classes* (New York: Putnam, 1877, 1879), and *Sun-Lighted Tenements: Thirty-Five Years' Experience as an Owner*, Publication No. 12 (National Housing Association, March 1912); and Robert A. M. Stern, Thomas Mellins, and David Fishman, *New York 1880: Architecture and Urbanism in the Gilded Age* (New York: Monacelli Press, 1999), 878–83. For Astral Apartments, see New York City Landmarks Preservation Commission "Astral Apartments" designation report prepared by James T. Dillon (1983); and Stern, *New York 1880*, 958–60. For City and Suburban Homes, see Veiller, "Tenement House Reform in New York City," 107–09; Plunz, *A History of Housing*, 99–103; Andrew S. Dolkart and Sharon Z. Macosko, *A Dream Fulfilled: City and Suburban's York Avenue Estate* (New York: Coalition to Save City & Suburban Housing, Inc., 1988); and New York City Landmarks Preservation Commission, "City and Suburban Homes Company, Avenue A (York Avenue) Estate" and "City and Suburban Homes Company, First Avenue Estate" designation reports prepared by Gail Harris (1990). For other model tenement projects, see Plunz, *A History of Housing*, 88–112.

14.   Anthony Jackson, *A Place Called Home: A History of Low-Cost Housing in Manhattan* (Cambridge, Mass.: MIT Press, 1976), 82–83; and Jared N. Day, *Urban Castles: Tenement Housing and Landlord Activism in New York City, 1890–1943* (New York: Columbia University Press, 1999), 31–56.

15.   *Laws of New York*, Chapter 356 (1862).

16.   The formation of the Citizens' Association has often been seen as a response to the New York City Draft Riots of July 1863; see Veiller, "Tenement House Reform in New York City," 93. Iver Bernstein, *The New York City Draft Riots: Their Significance for American Society and Politics* (New York: Oxford University Press, 1990), 68–69, discusses the reaction of the progressives, particularly the AICP, to the draft riots.

17.   Ford, *Slums and Housing*, 142.

18.   Citizens' Association of New York, *Report of the Council of Hygiene and Public Health of the Citizens' Association of New York, Upon the Sanitary Condition of the City* (New York: D. Appleton & Co., 1865). The association's survey report is discussed in Veiller, "Tenement House Reform," 92–94; Ford, *Slums and Housing*, 142–49; Lubove, *The Progressives and the*

Slums, 17–20; Plunz, *A History of Housing*, 21–22; and Gwendolyn Wright, *Building the Dream: A Social History of Housing in America* (New York: Pantheon, 1981), 118–19.

19.　Citizens' Association, *Report*, lxix. In 1860, New York City consisted only of Manhattan Island.

20.　In comparison to a building such as 97 Orchard Street, which housed twenty-two families, the figure of 7 1/6 families per tenement does not seem excessive. It must be remembered, however, that this survey was undertaken before the major wave of construction of new tenements. Thus, many of tenements that were recorded were small converted single-family houses.

21.　Citizens' Association, *Report*, lxx.

22.　Citizens' Association, *Report*, lxxii.

23.　J. T. Kennedy, "Report of the Eighth Sanitary Inspection District," in Citizens' Association, *Report*, 349.

24.　Kennedy, "Report," 91. In 1855 the Tenth Ward was forty-five percent German, up from twenty-six percent in 1845. The German population continued to increase after 1855; see Stanley Nadel, *Little Germany: Ethnicity, Religion, and Class in New York City, 1845–80* (Urbana: University of Chicago Press, 1990), 32.

25.　Kennedy, "Report," 91, 93.

26.　Consolidated Draft Lists, Class 1, Fifth District, N.Y., "Corrections of Enrollment, May and June 1864, Names Added A–K" (National Archives, Record Group 110, Washington, D.C.); research undertaken by Marsha Dennis.

27.　Forty-three foreign-born residents are recorded as being from Prussia, Bavaria, Wurttemberg, Baden, and Austria. There were also three residents from Russia (possibly Volga Germans), four from England, and one from Ireland. These figures for 1870 are from the second census enumeration of that year. In the first enumeration New York City claimed to have been grossly undercounted (only sixty-one people were recorded at 97 Orchard Street), and so the government commissioned a second enumeration. The 1880 Census also indicates a large German population.

28.　Kennedy, "Report," 93

29.　*United States Census*, 97 Orchard Street (1870).

30.　State of Ohio Department of Health, Division of Vital Statistics, Certificate of Death, Julius Gumpertz, February 2, 1924; research on Gumpertz in Cincinnati was supplied to the Tenement Museum by professional and amateur genealogists, including Mel Bashore, Sharon Hoyt,

Janet Kowal, Kay Heller Phillips, and Susan Stone.

31.   Information on the Gumpertz household from Tenement Museum Archives, New York City, Gumperts, RG 3.6.1, Gumpertz Folder; *A Tenement Story: The History of 97 Orchard Street and The Lower East Side Tenement Museum* (New York: Lower East Side Tenement Museum, 2004), 41–42; and "In the Matter of the Application of Natalie [sic] Gumpertz, For Letters of Administration on the Goods Chattels, and Credits of Julius Gumpertz Accounted Naturally Dead," Surrogates Court, City and County of New York, Petition & Affidavit, June 14, 1883.

32.   Kennedy, "Report," 93.

33.   Kennedy, "Report," 95–96 and *New Yorker Staats-Zeitung* May 19, 1872, 8.

34.   Georg Techla, *Drei Jahre in New* York (Zwichau: Verein zur Verbreitung Volksschriften, 1862), 100–101, quoted in Stanley Nadel, *Little Germany: Ethnicity, Religion, and Class in New York City, 1845–80* (Urbana: University of Chicago Press, 1990), 105.

35.   *New Yorker Staats-Zeitung* November 11, 1864.

36.   Lower East Side Tenement Museum, "Minding the Store Research Source Book," (2010), 3, 17–20.

37.   *New Yorker Staats-Zeitung* March 10, 1870 and January 21, 1873, 8; notice of the meeting appeared on January 20, 1873, 5. Information from research conducted by Britta Graf (Tenement Museum Archives, New York City, *New Yorker Staats-Zeitung*, RG 3.6.2, Folder 16).

38.   Jablonski Building Conservation, Inc., *Investigative Probes and Paint Archeology: Lower East Side Tenement Museum: Schneider Saloon 97 Orchard Street New York,* NY (2010), 2–4, 90.

39.   Jablonski, *Investigative Probes*, 87–88.

40.   According to genealogist Marsha Dennis, John Schneider's name first appears in the City Directory as an occupant of 97 Orchard Street in 1865. Information on Schneider in Tenement Museum Archives, New York City, RG 3.6.2, Schneider Folder.

41.   Researchers at the Tenement Museum have identified thirteen Irish households living at 97 Orchard Street between 1853 and 1935.

42.   United States Census (1870).

43.   For the Moore family, see Lower East Side Tenement Museum, "Irish Apartment Source Book" (2008); Tenement Museum Archives, New York City, RG 3.6.1, Moore Folder; and *A Tenement Story*, 40. The Moores had eight children, all girls, four of whom died before reaching adulthood. Bridget Moore died in childbirth in 1882, at the age of 36.

DESIGN AND CONSTRUCTION
OF 97 ORCHARD STREET

1.   The only streets in the Tenth Ward wider than fifty-four feet were Grand Street (seventy-five feet) and Canal Street (ninety feet).

2.   E. Robinson and R. H. Pidgeon, *Robinson's Atlas of the City of New York* (New York: E. Robinson, 1885), plate 5.

3.   At the time the 95–99 Orchard Street tenements were erected, there was only one other five-story building on the block, a rear building at no. 103 (demolished), which was probably a tenement.

4.   Edward Lubitz, "The Tenement Problem in New York City and the Movement for its Reform 1856–1867" (PhD diss., New York University, 1970), 319–20.

5.   *Annual Report of the Superintendent of Buildings* (New York: Department of Buildings, 1863), 77; (1864), 123. Besides the fifty-five tenements begun in 1863, only three other buildings were erected in the Tenth Ward. In 1864, five other buildings were erected.

6.   James D. McCabe, Jr., *Lights and Shadows of New York Life; or, the Sights and Sensations of the Great City* (Philadelphia: National Publishing Company, 1872), 686, 689.

7.   Biographical information on Glockner was uncovered by genealogist Marsha Dennis, Tenement Museum Archives, New York City, Glockner Folder. An investigation of the construction of tenements that line that portion of Orchard Street located in the Tenth Ward shows a mix of buildings erected by individuals involved with only a single structure and those built in larger groups. There are several instances where a single owner erected one row of adjacent buildings; owner/builder A. Dooper erected the four tenements at 27–33 Orchard Street in 1871. Only one major developer seems to have been active on the street: Frederick Heerlein, who, by himself or in the partnerships of Folz & Heerlein and Heerlein & Rabinstein, was responsible for the construction of thirteen tenements (nos. 70–78, 118, 132–138, and 133–37), all designed by William Jose in 1872–73. In 1873, Heerlein is listed in city directories as an upholsterer living on Eldridge Street. In the following year, he is listed as a builder at 138 Orchard Street.

8.   United States Census (1870); also see *A Tenement Story: The History of 97 Orchard Street and The Lower East Side Tenement Museum* (New York: Lower East Side Tenement Museum, 2004), 39.

9.   Following Glockner's sale in 1886, the property changed hands

many times until the Helpern family purchased it in 1919; the Helperns sold the building to the Lower East Side Tenement Museum in 1996.

10.   Glockner's tenements on Allen Street were designed by Theodore J. Bier. Bier's name first appears in city directories in 1861, where he is listed as an architect with an office at 66 Norfolk Street on the Lower East Side. Through 1884, when he moved to Brooklyn, Bier's office was located in various Lower East Side buildings; see Dennis Francis, *Architects in Practice in New York City, 1840–1900* (New York: Committee for the Preservation of Architectural Records, 1980), 16. Since Bier was active on the Lower East Side as early as 1861, it is possible that Glockner had previously hired him as the architect of 97 Orchard Street.

11.   Architects and architectural firms active on Orchard Street in the nineteenth century include Theodore J. Bier, Leopold Biela, Julius Boekell, Louis Burger, Frederick Ebeling, William Graul, Herter Brothers, Frederick Jenth, William Jose (by far, the most active architect on the street, designing at least fifteen tenements), Rentz & Lange, Frank Schuck, and William Taft. Many of these architects were German. Several of the architects had their offices on the Lower East Side.

12.   For a detailed discussion of Italianate style as it appeared on New York City's row houses and mansions, see Charles Lockwood, "The Italianate Dwelling House in New York City," *Journal of the Society of Architectural Historians* 31 (May 1972): 145–51; and Charles Lockwood, *Bricks and Brownstone: The New York Row House, 1783–1929, An Architectural and Social History* (New York: McGraw-Hill, 1972; reprinted, New York: Rizzoli, 2003), 125–225.

13.   The construction of five-story and raised basement tenements appears to have been fairly common during the 1860s; other examples can be seen on Orchard Street (no. 96) and on other streets on the Lower East Side. Other five-story tenements from the 1860s, such as no. 95 Orchard Street, dispense with the raised basement; by the early 1870s, this form had become the predominant type of tenement erected in the Tenth Ward.

14.   Historic Preservation & Illumination, "Paint Analysis Report" (2004, Tenement Museum Archives, New York City), 12. Historic Preservation & Illumination and its predecessor firm, Acroterion Historic Preservation Consultants, undertook extensive analysis of the interior paint at 97 Orchard Street in 1992–97.

15.   The 1862 "act to provide for the Regulation and Inspection of Buildings, the more effectual prevention of fires, and the better preserva-

tion of life and property in the City of New York," (*Laws of New York*, Chapter 356) which established the New York City Department of Building, also regulated the use of wood cornices. According to this law, wood cornices could be used only on buildings up to forty feet in height and on three-story and basement dwellings. Since 97 Orchard Street is fifty-eight feet high, a wood cornice was not permitted. No. 96 Orchard Street, erected in 1866 across the street from no. 97, has an identical cornice. The facade of no. 96 is very similar to those at 97–99 Orchard Street, except that, in place of the brownstone lintels and sills, no. 96 has cast-iron elements that are well preserved. The color of the cornice at 97 Orchard Street was established by paint analysis; see Historic Preservation & Illumination, "Paint Analysis," 12.

16. An archaeological excavation uncovered stone paving two feet below the modern grade; see Joan H. Geismar, "Archaeological Evaluation: The Lower East Side Tenement Museum," report prepared for the Lower East Side Tenement Museum, 1999, revised 2003, 2.

17. Hugh Bonner and Lawrence Veiller, "Tenement House Fires in New York," in Robert W. DeForest and Lawrence Veiller, eds., *The Tenement House Problem*, vol. 1 (New York: Macmillan, 1903), 287.

18. *Laws of New York*, Chapter 334, Section 29 (1901). The 1901 law that banned fire ladders also permitted steel rope ladders in buildings of up to three stories; see Roy Lubove, *The Progressives and the Slums: Tenement House Reform in New York City 1890–1917* (Pittsburgh: University of Pittsburgh Press, 1962), 136.

19. A party-wall balcony was only possible for nos. 97 and 99 Orchard Street because they share a party wall and have identical floor and window heights. Nos. 95 and 97 Orchard Street have differing floor and window heights.

20. "Health and Profit," *New York Times*, November 29, 1896, 13.

21. Bonner and Veiller, "Tenement House Fires," 262.

22. Hugh Bonner and Lawrence Veiller, "Tenement House Fire-Escapes in New York and Brooklyn," in DeForest and Veiller, *The Tenement House Problem*, vol. 1, 288.

23. The plan of a building such as 97 Orchard Street was illustrated as typical of tenements erected after 1850 in James Ford, *Slums and Housing* (Cambridge, Mass.: Harvard University Press, 1936), Appendix by I. N. Phelps Stokes, plate I.

24. Island House Wrights Corporation, "Preliminary Conditions Re-

port for the Main Staircase at 97 Orchard Street," March 25, 2005 (Tenement Museum Archives, New York City).

25. Historic Preservation & Illumination, "Paint Analysis," 3.

26. Historic Preservation & Illumination, "Paint Analysis," 6.

27. Jablonski Berkowitz Conservation, Inc., "Conservation Treatment Plan" (2006; Tenement Museum Archives, New York City).

28. Historic Preservation & Illumination, "Paint Analysis," 3; Jablonski Building Conservation, "Investigative Probes," 73–74. For distemper, see Jablonski Building Conservation, "Investigative probes," 74–75.

29. Historic Preservation & Illumination, "Paint Analysis," 7–8.

30. *Report of the Conditions of Tenant Houses in New York* (1857), 34; quoted in Lubitz, "The Tenement Problem in New York City," 81–82.

31. Initially, it was assumed that these windows had been cut into the walls between the kitchens and bedrooms later in the nineteenth century. However, paint analysis shows that the graining on the enframements of these windows is nearly identical to that on the baseboards and other original woodwork. The conclusion is that the window frames are either original or were installed shortly after the building was completed; see, Historic Preservation & Illumination, "Paint Analysis," 8.

32. Citizens' Association of New York. *Report of the Council of Hygiene and Public Health of the Citizens' Association of New York, Upon the Sanitary Condition of the City* (New York: D. Appleton & Co., 1865), 94. For the Croton Water system, see Charles H. Weidner, *Water for a City: A History of New York City's Problem from the Beginning to the Delaware River System* (New Brunswick: Rutgers University Press, 1973); *The Old Croton Aqueduct: Rural Resources Meet Urban Needs* (Yonkers: Hudson River Museum, 1992); and Gerard T. Koeppel, *Water for Gotham: A History* (Princeton: Princeton University Press, 2000).

33. *Annual Report of the Croton Aqueduct Department 1863* (New York: Croton Water Department, 1864), 59; cited in Geismar, "Archaeological Evaluation," 5.

34. Geismar, "Archaeological Evaluation," 4–5.

35. Tenement toilet facilities are discussed in detail in Albert L. Webster, "Tenement House Sanitation," in DeForest and Veiller, *The Tenement House Problem*, vol. 1, 303–27. Information on the toilet facilities at 97 Orchard Street is detailed in Lower East Side Tenement Museum, "Rear Yard of 97 Orchard Street Source Book" (2009); the location and form of the backyard toilets was confirmed during the archaeological investigation

of the property undertaken of 1999 (see Geismar, "Archaeological Evaluation," 5).

36.   Albert L. Webster, "Tenement House Sanitation," in DeForest and Veiller, *The Tenement House Problem*, vol. 1, 307.

37.   Geismar, "Archaeological Evaluation," 5; Webster, "Tenement House Sanitation," 307–08. Water from the hydrant may have been supplemented by rain water drained off the tenement's roof and channeled through a simple stone and brick box drain. Since the force of the flushing water was often inadequate to actually clean the waste trough, it was often the additional force and volume contributed by the rain runoff that actually washed out the vault.

38.   Geismar, "Archaeological Evaluation," 4.

39.   J. T. Kennedy, "Report of the Eighth Sanitary Inspection District," in Citizens' Association, *Report*, 92.

40.   Citizens' Association, *Report*, 95.

41.   "The Streets of New York," *New York Tribune*, September 19, 1963. This excerpt is part of a description of the Eleventh Ward to the northeast of the Tenth Ward, but such garbage-boxes were common throughout the tenement neighborhoods.

42.   Evidence is inconclusive as to whether the shutters and enclosure boards are original or were added shortly after the tenement was completed. The fireplaces appear not to have been heavily used.

43.   The stoves are discussed in "Life in the Tenements: Conditions on the Swarming East Side," *Real Estate Record and Builders Guide* 67 (February 16, 1901): 278. The Citizens' Association, *Report*, 94, notes that "stoves are principally used for giving warmth as well as for culinary purposes."

44.   Lawrence Veiller, "Tenement House Rentals," in DeForest and Veiller, *The Tenement House Problem*, vol. 2, appendix 9, 439–58.

45.   Henry Rosenthal, interview, Tenement Museum Archives, New York City, RG 3.6.1, Rogarshevsky Folder; *A Tenement Story*, 45.

46.   Confino Resource Book, prepared by Vicki Grubman, Tenement Museum Archives, New York City, RG 3.6.1, Confino Folder; *A Tenement Story*, 47.

47.   "The Family of Morris & Beckie Abrams," prepared by Vicki Grubman, Tenement Museum Archives, New York City, RG 3.6.1, Abrams Folder, 6.

48.   Josephine Baldizzi Esposito, interview, Tenement Museum Archives, New York City, RG 3.6.1, Baldizzi Folder, 70.

49.   *Reports of the Industrial Commission on Immigration and on Education*, vol. 15 of the Commission's Reports (Washington, D.C.: Government Printing Office, 1901), xxix, 369–70. According to the report, 95 percent of garment finishing was undertaken by Italian women.

50.   "Tenement-House Work and Legislation Regarding It," in *Reports of the Industrial Commission*, 373.

51.   *Annual Report of the Factory Inspectors of the State of New York*, vols. 1–15 (Albany: Factory Inspectors of the State of New York, 1887–1915). The issue of tenement house factories is analyzed in Eileen Boris, *Home To Work: Motherhood and the Politics of Industrial Homework in the United States* (New York: Cambridge University Press, 1994).

52.   *Annual Report of the Factory Inspectors* vol. 7 (1892), 14.

53.   *Laws of New York*, Chapter 409 (1886), amended Chapter 673 (1892), Section 13.

54.   "Tenement-House Work and Legislation Regarding It," in *Reports of the Industrial Commission*, 373.

55.   *Annual Report of the Factory Inspectors*, vols. 1–15 (1887–1915).

56.   The *Annual Report of the Factory Inspector*, vol. 7 (1892), 15, notes that "with the present force it is not possible to inspect all these places with any degree of frequency."

57.   *Annual Report of the Factory Inspector*, vol. 7 (1892), 165, where the name is incorrectly spelled "Harry Levin." For the Levines, see Tenement Museum Archives, New York City, RG 3.6.1, Levine Folder; *A Tenement Story*, 97.

58.   *Annual Report of the Factory Inspector*, vol. 10 (1895), where name is misspelled "Harriz Levine."

59.   Tenement Museum Archives, New York City, RG 3.6.1, Levine Folder; *A Tenement Story*, 97.

60.   *Annual Report of the Factory Inspector*, vol. 15 (1900), 34.

61.   "Heat Record Broken; Twenty-Three Dead," *New York Times* July 19, 1905, 1.

62.   Esposito, interview, 58.

63.   Seymour Gottesman, interview, Tenement Museum Archives, New York City, RG 3.6.1, Box 1, Gottesman Folder.

64.   Robert Shackleton, *The Book of New York* (Philadelphia: The Penn Publishing Company, 1917), 110.

65.   Moses King, ed., *King's How To See New York: A Complete Trustworthy Guide Book* (Boston: Moses King, 1914), 84.

66.   Esposito, interview, 87.

NEW TENEMENT LAWS AND THE CHANGING
CHARACTER OF THE LOWER EAST SIDE
AND ITS TENEMENTS

1.   *Laws of New York*, Chapter 908 (1867). The 1867 law is discussed in Lawrence Veiller, "Tenement House Reform in New York City," in William DeForest and Lawrence Veiller, eds., *The Tenement House Problem* (New York: Macmillan, 1903), 94–97; James Ford, *Slums and Housing* (Cambridge, Mass.: Harvard University Press, 1936), 154–55; Anthony Jackson, *A Place Called Home: A History of Low-Cost Housing in Manhattan* (Cambridge, Mass.: MIT Press, 1976), 31–34; Roy Lubove, *The Progressives and the Slums: Tenement House Reform in New York City 1890–1917* (Pittsburgh: University of Pittsburgh Press, 1962), 25–28; Richard Plunz, *A History of Housing in New York City: Dwelling Type and Social Change in the American Metropolis* (New York: Columbia University Press, 1990), 22; and Robert A. M. Stern, Thomas Mellins, and David Fishman, *New York 1880: Architecture and Urbanism in the Gilded Age* (New York: Monacelli Press, 1999), 501.

2.   Ford, *Slums and Housing*, 155.

3.   *Laws of New York*. Chapter 504 (1879). This law is discussed in Veiller, "Tenement House Reform," 99–104; Ford, *Slums and Housing*, 164; Jackson, *A Place Called Home*, 61–62; Lubove, *The Progressives and the Slums*, 30–32; Plunz, *A History of Housing*, 24–27; and Stern, *New York 1880*, 504–05.

4.   Veiller, "Tenement House Reform," 100–02; and Plunz, *A History of Housing*, 24–28.

5.   Robert W. DeForest and Lawrence Veiller, "The Tenement House Problem," in DeForest and Veiller, *The Tenement House Problem*, 13–14.

6.   "Prize Tenements," *New York Times*, March 16, 1879, 6; cited in Lubove, *The Progressives and the Slums*, 32.

7.   "Report of the Committee," *Plumber and Sanitary Engineer* 2 (March 1879): 90.

8.   *Reports of the Industrial Commission on Immigration and on Education*, vol. 15 of the Commission's Reports (Washington, D.C.: Government Printing Office, 1901), 465, 469; quoted in Ford, *Slums and Housing*, 183.

9.   The federal census of 1890 was lost in a fire. A New York City police census from 1890 provides population data, but no information about nativity (New York City Municipal Archives).

10.   Jared N. Day, *Urban Castles: Tenement Housing and Landlord Activism in New York City, 1890–1943* (New York: Columbia University Press, 1999), 32–34.

11.　New York City Department of Finance, Conveyance Books, block 414, lot 22 (New York City Department of Finance, Office of Real Property).

12.　Donna R. Gabaccia, *From Sicily to Elizabeth Street: Housing and Social Change Among Italian Immigrants 1880–1930* (Albany: State University of New York Press, 1984), 74.

13.　Lower East Side Tenement Museum, "Minding the Store," 5–6, 57–58. In 1898, when newly naturalized Israel Lustgarten registered to vote, he gave his address as 97 Orchard Street "store level"; see Voter Registration Lists, New York County, 1898 (New York City Department of Records, Municipal Archives); United States Census (1900).

14.　Lower East Side Tenement Museum, "Minding the Store," 60; Jeffrey S. Gurock, "Kosher Butchers of the 19th Century," in "Minding the Store," 68–69; and Paula E. Hyman, "Immigrant Women and Consumer Protest: The New York City Kosher Meat Boycott of 1902," *American Jewish History* 70 (September 1980), 91–105. The photograph of Lustgarten's damaged store front is in *New York World* May 17, 1902 (Evening Edition), 3.

15.　Historic Preservation & Illumination, "Paint Analysis" (2004, Tenement Museum Archives, New York City), 4–7.

16.　Historic Preservation & Illumination, "Paint Analysis," 2.

17.　In 1898, the *New York Times* reported that wallpaper rolls could be acquired for between four cents and two dollars.

18.　*Laws of New York*, Chapter 567, Section 6 (1895).

19.　Gwendolyn Wright, *Building the Dream: A Social History of Housing in America* (New York: Pantheon, 1981), 132.

20.　Analysis of the wallpaper at 97 Orchard Street was completed by paper conservator Reba Fishman Snyder in 1994 and 1997, with additional research undertaken on the basement in 2010; see "Wallpaper Analysis Report" (1997; Tenement Museum Archive, New York City) and "Wallpaper Sampling and Survey, Lower East Side Tenement Museum: Schneider Saloon Basement Level 97 Orchard Street New York, NY 10002" (2010). Parlors had up to twenty-two layers of paper. Snyder's analysis documents that the parlors were repapered approximately every two or three years; see page 13.

21.　For linoleum, see Jane Powell, *Linoleum* (Salt Lake City: Gibbs Smith, 2003); Leo Blackman and Deborah Dietsch, "A New Look at Linoleum," *Old House Journal* 10 (January 1982): 9–12; and Bonnie Wehle Parks Snyder, "Linoleum," in Thomas J. Jester, ed., *Twentieth Century Building Materials* (New York: McGraw-Hill, 1995).

22.　"Life in the Tenements" and "Conditions on the Swarming East

Side," *Real Estate Record and Builders Guide* 67 (February 16, 1901): 276.

23.   Elizabeth Emery, "Wall Hangings: Their Comparative Cost, Beauty and Durability," *House Beautiful* 19 (May 1906): 17; "Stencil Work on Burlap," *Wall Paper News and Interior Decorator* 29 (June 1907): 25.

24.   The gold leaf was discovered as a result of paint analysis undertaken by Susan Buck (2002, Tenement Museum Archives, New York City).

25.   Jablonski Berkowitz Conservation, Inc., "Architectural Conservation of the First Floor Hallway Lower East Side Tenement Museum" (1997; Tenement Museum Archives, New York City); a similar redesigned hallway is illustrated in *Fourth Report of the Tenement House Department of the City of New York* (New York: Tenement House Department, 1907–08), 137.

26.   Historic Preservation & Illumination, "Paint Analysis," 11. A resource for metal ceilings is Mary B. Dierickx, "Leaves of Iron: Stamped Metal Ornament," *The Journal of Decorative and Propaganda Arts* 9 (Summer 1988): 44–59. Because the dies for creating the patterns on metal ceilings were continuously reused, it is impossible to date the various patterns.

THE 1901 TENEMENT HOUSE ACT AND THE TENEMENT HOUSE DEPARTMENT

1.   "Health and Profit," *New York Times*, November 29, 1896, 13.

2.   Lawrence Veiller, "Tenement House Reform in New York City, 1834–1900," in Robert E. DeForest and Lawrence Veiller, eds., *The Tenement House Problem*, vol. 1 (New York: Macmillan, 1903), 109.

3.   Veiller, "Tenement House Reform," 109.

4.   "Building Code Attacked," *New York Times*, September 23, 1899, 5.

5.   Roy Lubove, *The Progressives and the Slums: Tenement House Reform in New York City 1890–1917* (Pittsburgh: University of Pittsburgh Press, 1962), 120–21.

6.   Veiller, "Tenement House Reform," 111.

7.   *Charities* 3 (July 29, 1899): 1.

8.   "Tenement House Show," *New York Times*, February 10, 1900, 7; "For Housing the Poor," *Chicago Tribune*, February 11, 1900, 5; Veiller, "Tenement House Reform," 111–13; Lubove, *Progressives and the Slums*, 122–23.

9.   Richard Plunz, *A History of Housing in New York City: Dwelling Type and Social Change in the American Metropolis* (New York: Columbia University Press, 1990): 44–46; also illustrated in DeForest and Veiller, *The*

Tenement House Problem, vol. 1, opposite 10 and 112.

10.   *Laws of New York*, Chapter 279 (1900). This law is discussed in "The Proceedings of the Commission," DeForest and Veiller, *The Tenement House Problem*, vol. 2, 93–94; and in "The Tenement-House Commission Act," *Charities* 4 (April 21, 1900): 4. The politics involved in the passage of this law are discussed in Lubove, *The Progressives and the Slums*, 125–26.

11.   "The Tenement Commission," *New York Times*, April 17, 1900, 6.

12.   "The Tenement Commission," 6; "The Tenement-House Commission," *Charities* 4 (April 21, 1900): 1.

13.   A synopsis of the commission's work appears in "The Proceedings of the Commission," 93–100, and is discussed in Lubove, *The Progressives and the Slums*, 132–39.

14.   "Tenement Commission Makes Its Report," *New York Times*, February 26, 1901, 7.

15.   "The Proposed Code of Tenement House Laws," in DeForest and Veiller, *The Tenement House Problem*, vol. 2, 103–46; "The Act for the Creation of a Separate Tenement House Department," DeForest and Veiller, *The Tenement House Problem*, vol. 2, 149–59.

16.   "The Tenement Houses," (editorial), *New York Times*, April 11, 1901, 8.

17.   "The Tenement House Commission's Bills," *Real Estate Record and Builders Guide* 67 (March 2, 1901): 349.

18.   "The Tenement House Commission's Bills," 349–50.

19.   *Laws of New York*, Chapter 334 (1901). The entire proceedings of the Tenement House Commission and its proposed tenement house act are reprinted in DeForest and Veiller, "The Proceedings of the Commission," vol. 2, 91–146.

20.   "Building Department Stormed," *New York Tribune*, April 7, 1901, 5.

21.   "Tenement Law Violated," *New York Tribune*, July 23, 1901, 1; "Mr. Bernstein's Reply," *New York Tribune*, July 24, 1901, 7; "Tenement Law Evaded, Says Mr. De Forest," *New York Times*, July 23, 1901, 2.

22.   Ford, *Slums and Housing* (Cambridge, Mass: Harvard University Press, 1936), 205

23.   For the Progressive Era, see Paul Boyer, *Urban Masses and Moral Order in America, 1820–1920* (Cambridge, Mass.: Harvard University Press, 1978); also see Diane Ravitch, *The Great School Wars New York City, 1805–1973: A History of the Public Schools as Battlefield of Social Change* (New York: Basic Books, 1974); Allan Freeman Davis, *Spearheads for Reform: The So-*

cial Settlements and the Progressive Movement, 1890–1914 (New York: Oxford University Press, 1967); and Mina Carson, *Settlement Folk: Social Thought and the American Settlement Movement, 1885–1930* (Chicago: University of Chicago Press, 1990).

24. The law did not ban construction of tenements on twenty-five foot wide lots, but made it inefficient to build such structures. Still, there were examples of tenements constructed on these narrow lots, although they were required to occupy less of the lot area and had more generous shafts and courts.

25. New law tenement plans are analyzed in Plunz, *A History of Housing,* 48–49.

26. *New York Tribune* editorials: "The Tenement House Report," February 27, 1901, 6; "Wise Moderation," March 6, 1901, 6; "A Moderate Tenement House Reform," April 10, 1901, 6; "The New Tenement House Law," June 29, 1901, 6.

27. *Laws of New York*, Chapter 466 (1901).

28. Adolph Bloch, "History of Tenement House Legislation," *Real Estate Record and Builders Guide* 84 (July 21, 1909): 227.

29. United Real Estate Owners' Association, "The Tenement House Law of the City of New York," pamphlet, collection of The New York Public Library (1901), preface.

30. "The Tenement House Law"; also see "New Tenement Law," *Real Estate Record and Builders Guide* 67 (June 29, 1901): 1136.

31. "Tenement House Law," *Real Estate Record and Builders Guide* 68 (July 6, 1901): 2.

32. "Tenement House Law Violently Attacked," *New York Times*, September 13, 1901, 12.

33. "Tenement Evils as Seen by the Tenants: Testimony of a Tenant [Mr. Henry Moscowitz]," in DeForest and Veiller, *The Tenement House Problem*, vol. 1, 414.

34. *Laws of New York*, Chapter 334, Section 80 (1901).

35. In 1902, a Tenement House Department inspector completed an I-card (improvement card) for 97 Orchard Street indicating that as of July 10, 1902, there were glass door-panels on all of the doors on the second through fourth floors (New York City Department of Housing, Preservation and Development, Code Violations Division). No mention is made of the fifth-floor doors. Windows were not placed in the doors of the front apartments on the first floor, since these apartments had been converted for commercial use. Thus the only surviving, entirely intact, original hall door

at 97 Orchard Street is that leading to the store on the north side of the hall.

36.   *Laws of New York*, Chapter 334, Section 83 (1901). A survey of the building undertaken in 1902 records an inadequate skylight; see "I-card, 97 Orchard Street."

37.   *Laws of New York*, Chapter 334, Section 82 (1901).

38.   Information on the American Gas Reduction Company based on a report prepared for the Lower East Side Tenement Museum, by Frank Biebel (Tenement Museum Archives, New York City, 1995).

39.   Max Mason, "We Came to the Lower East Side," typescript, Tenement Museum Archives, New York City, RG 3.6.1, Box 2, 6.

40.   Elizabeth Ewen, *Immigrant Women in the Land of Dollars: Life and Culture on the Lower East Side, 1890–1925* (New York: Monthly Review Press, 1985), 152.

41.   Tenement House Department of the City of New York, *First Report of the Tenement House Department of the City of New York*, vol. 1 (New York: Tenement House Department, 1903), 85–86.

42.   *Laws of New York*, Chapter 334, Section 79 (1901).

43.   "Tenement House Law," *Real Estate Record and Builders Guide* 68 (July 6, 1901): 2.

44.   All articles entitled "Ante-New Law Tenements," *Real Estate Record and Builders Guide* [editorial], 68 (October 5, 1901): 403; letter in response from Lawrence Veiller plus editorial rebuttal, 68 (October 19, 1901): 489–91; article with cost estimates and letter from realty firm, 68 (October 26, 1901): 530–32; reply from Lawrence Veiller, 68 (November 9. 1901): 611–12; article with cost estimates and letter in response to Veiller, 68 (November 23, 1901): 689.

45.   "Will Fight To Repeal Tenement House Law," *New York Times*, October 13, 1901, 24.

46.   *Laws of New York*, Chapter 179, Section 415 (1903).

47.   Editorial, *Real Estate Record and Builders Guide* 70 (July 12, 1902): 37.

48.   Analysis of paint layers on the window frames of the kitchen/ parlor windows suggests that these windows were cut through in the mid-1890s; see Historic Preservation & Illumination, "Paint Analysis Report" (2004, Tenement Museum Archives, New York City), 7.

49.   *Laws of New York*, Chapter 334, Section 100 (1901).

50.   *Laws of New York*, Chapter 334, Section 100 (1901).

51.   *Laws of New York*, Chapter 352, Section 100 (1902).

52.   The Moeschen case is discussed in Judith A. Gilbert, "Tenements

and Takings: *Tenement House Department of New York v. Moeschen* as a Counterpoint to *Lochner v. New York*," *Fordham Urban Law Journal* (Spring 1991): 437–505, and Felice Batlan, "A Reevaluation of the New York Court of Appeals: The Home, The Market, and Labor, 1885–1905," *Law and Social Inquiry* (Summer 2002): 503–07.

53.   "Tenement House Law Attacked," *Real Estate Record and Builders Guide* 71 (June 20, 1903): 1223.

54.   For the court decisions, see *Tenement House Department of City of New York v. Moeschen*, 84 N.Y. Supp. 577 (Supreme Court, Appellate Term, November 6, 1903); 89 App. Div. 526 (Supreme Court, Appellate Division, First Department, January 8, 1904); 179 N.Y. Rep. 325 (Court of Appeals, November 15, 1904); 203 U.S. 93 (United States Supreme Court, November 12, 1906).

55.   Tenement House Department, *Third Report* (1906), 139.

56.   Three buildings along Orchard Street in the Tenth Ward were altered in 1902 and two in 1903.

57.   New York City Department of Buildings, Borough of Manhattan. Alteration Application No. 2105-1905.

58.   The 1902 I-card shows the original dimensions of the kitchen and parlor, indicating that the wall was shifted after 1902. The relocation of the walls is evident on a plan submitted to the New York City Department of Buildings as part of Alteration Application 2105-05.

59.   Dennis Steadman Francis, *Architects in Practice in New York City 1840–1899* (New York: Committee for the Preservation of Architectural Records, 1980), 64; James Ward, *Architects in Practice New York City 1900–1940* (New York: Committee for the Preservation of Architectural Records, 1989), 64.

60.   Landmark Facilities Group, Utilities Survey of 97 Orchard Street (2005; Tenement Museum Archives, New York City), concludes that the water pipes leading to the apartments and those for the toilets are identical.

61.   *Laws of New York,* Chapter 84 (1887).

62.   *The Health Department of the City of New York v. The Rector, Church Wardens and Vestrymen of Trinity Church in the City of New York*, 145 N.Y. 32 (N.Y. Ct. of App. 1895); "The Supply of Water to Tenements," *Real Estate Record and Builders Guide* 55 (March 16, 1895): 412.

63.   The water pipes were manufactured by the Monitor Iron Works, a firm that was incorporated in May 1864. In 1892, the E.G. Blakslee Manufacturing Co., which manufactured iron pipe, changed its name to Monitor Iron Works. Apparently Monitor only began manufacturing water pipes af-

ter it became involved with the Blakslee firm. Information on the Monitor and Blakslee companies based on research prepared by Frank Biebel (1994; Tenement Museum Archives, New York City).

64. Landmark Facilities Group, Utilities Survey of 97 Orchard Street.

65. *Catalogue of the Alberene Stone Company* (1899–1900; Columbia University, Avery Library), plate 103. All Alberene fixtures contained a trademark plate, which was placed on the front face of the laundry tubs.

66. Mason, "We Came to the Lower East Side," 6.

67. The drawings that accompany Otto Reissmann's alteration permit of 1905 seem to show already extant sinks in each apartment; see New York City Department of Buildings, Alteration Application 2105-05.

68. The drawings accompanying Alteration Application 2105-05 show apartments at the rear of the first floor. The first-floor stores probably were extended back in the 1930s when all of the apartments in the building were vacated.

69. Historic Preservation & Illumination, "Paint Analysis," 12.

70. The politics of DeForest's appointment are discussed in Lubove, *The Progressives and the Slums*, 153–55.

71. Mary B. Sayles, quoted in Tenement House Department, *First Report,* vol. 1, 116.

72. Tenement House Department, *First Report*, vol. 1, 53.

73. The I-cards are discussed in Tenement House Department, *First Report*, vol. 1, 53–57. The cards are now available on line at www.nyc.gov/html/hpd/html/home/home.shtml, accessed December 7, 2011.

74. Joan Geismar, "Archaeological Evaluation," (1999/1903) in *Lower East Side Tenement Museum Historic Structures* Report (2003), 2

75. Tenement House Committee of the Charity Organization Society of the City of New York, *Housing Reform in New York City* (New York: Charity Organization Society, 1914), 2.

THE CHANGING CHARACTER OF THE LOWER EAST SIDE IN THE EARLY TWENTIETH CENTURY

1. The survey was published in Tenement House Department of the City of New York, *First Report of the Tenement House Department of the City of New York*, vol. 2 (New York: Tenement House Department, 1903).

2. "10th Ward Nativity," map in Tenement House Department, *First Report*, vol. 2, insert.

3.   "Ward 10. Tenement House Population. Nativity and Parentage of Heads of Families," chart in Tenement House Department, *First Report*, vol . 2, 46–47.

4.   "Ward Summary—Total Population. Nativity and Parentage of Heads of Families," Tenement House Department, *First Report*, vol. 2, 103.

5.   "Ward 10. Tenement House Population. Number of Families Having Given Number of Persons," Tenement House Department, *First Report*, vol. 2, 115.

6.   Population statistics from United States Census, 1880, 1900, and 1910, and from New York City Police Census, 1890 (New York City Municipal Archives).

7.   Dora Meltzer, handbill, Tenement Museum Archives, New York City, RG 3.6.1, Melzer Folder; several copies of Meltzer's handbill advertisement were discovered beneath floor boards on the second floor of 97 Orchard Street. Dora lived in the apartment of her brother Hyman and his wife Bessie in the early years of the twentieth century.

8.   Henry Rosenthal, interview, May 17, 1998, Tenement Museum Archives, New York City, RG 3.6.1, Rogarshevsky Folder; *A Tenement Story: The History of 97 Orchard Street and the Lower East Side Tenement Museum* (New York: Lower East Side Tenement Museum, 2004), 46–48; 51; Josephine Baldizzi Esposito, interview, Tenement Museum Archives, New York City, RG 3.6.1, Baldizzi Folder, 3–4.

9.   Displacement was not an issue of concern to most people in the late nineteenth century. In fact, an effort was made to site the parks on particularly overcrowded areas. In March 1896, the Board of Health announced that it had chosen as a site for Hamilton Fish Park a location that "would give an open air space in the most crowded locality and will remove the greatest number of conditions which may have become a menace to the public health" (*New York Times*, March 25, 1896, 9). The 1890 Police Census gives some idea of the number of people displaced for the construction of parks. According to this census, 3,568 people lived on the two square blocks that later in the decade were cleared for Hamilton Fish Park; and 3,025 people lived on the three oddly shaped blocks that became Seward Park. For additional information on Hamilton Fish Park, see New York City Landmarks Preservation Commission, "Hamilton Fish Park Play Center," designation report prepared by Andrew S. Dolkart (New York: Landmarks Preservation Commission, 1982); for the issue of displacement due to the construction of parks and other amenities, see

"Life in the Tenements: Conditions on the Swarming East Side," *Real Estate Record and Builders Guide* 67 (February 16, 1901): 276; and "East Side Real Estate," *Real Estate Record and Builders Guide* 72 (November 7, 1903): 824.

10. The idea for widening Delancey Street 150 feet on its south side, east of the Bowery, was first presented in 1901. Plans were formally adopted in 1903 and condemnation proceedings began in that year. This project entailed the destruction of three tenements erected in the 1870s at 109–13 Orchard Street, tenements at 108 and 114 Allen Street that had been built in 1866, and the entire Delancey Street frontage. For displacement due to construction of the Williamsburg Bridge approach, see "The Delancey Street Hegira," *Real Estate Record and Builders Guide* 68 (July 27, 1901): 120. Allen Street was a particularly unpleasant street on which to live, since the Second Avenue Elevated, built in 1879–80, ran up the center of the street. Elevated service ceased on June 12, 1942, and the line was dismantled for the World War II scrap steel drive. For Allen Street, see Juliette Dellecker Michaelson, "Allen Street and the 'Park Avenue of the Plain People,'" *Urban* 7 (Spring 2004): 10–12.

11. "The Delancey Street Hegira."

12. *Standard Bathroom and Plumbing Fixtures Catalogue P* (Pittsburgh: Standard Sanitary Manufacturing Co., 1911), 425, plate 6801 (Columbia University, Avery Library).

13. Rosenthal, interview.

14. Esposito, interview, 77.

15. *New York State Census* (1915).

16. Confino Resource Book, prepared by Vicki Grubman, Tenement Museum Archives, New York City, RG 3.6.1., Confino Folder; *A Tenement Story*, 47–48.

17. *United States Census* (1915); "A Quick Explanation of Ladino (Judeo-Spanish)," Ladino Preservation Council (www.sephardicstudies.org/quickladino.html), August 2011.

18. For Romaniote Jewish communities, see Rae Dalvin, *The Jews of Ioannina* (Philadelphia: Cadmus Press, 1990) and Nicholas P. Stravroulakis and Timothy J. DeVinney, *Jewish Sites and Synagogues of Greece* (Athens: Talos Press, 1991). The Romaniote synagogue, Kehila Kadosha Janina, is located about a block from 97 Orchard Street, at 280 Broome Street; see New York City Landmarks Preservation Commission, "Kehila Kadosha Janina Synagogue Designation Report," report prepared by Virginia Kurshan (New York: Landmarks Preservation Commission, 2004).

19.   "The Family of Morris & Beckie Abrams," typescript, Tenement Museum Archives, New York City, RG 3.6.1. Abrams Folder.

20.   *A Tenement Story*, 51.

21.   New York State Census (1925).

22.   "Manhattan Apartment Vacancies by Census Tract," *Real Estate Record and Builders Guide* 132 (August 5, 1933): 6. The issue of vacancy rates is discussed in Suzanne Rachel Wassermann, *The Good Old Days of Poverty: The Battle Over the Fate of New York City's Lower East Side During the Depression* (Ph.D. diss., New York University, 1990).

23.   *Laws of New York*, Chapter 526 (1934).

24.   Evidence for residence as late as June 1935 is the fact that a calendar was found in one apartment displaying that month.

25.   City of New York, Department of Housing and Buildings, Division of Housing, Vacancy Report, October 11, 1935; New York City Department of Housing, Preservation, and Development, "Post Cycle Survey," December 14, 1930.

26.   "Lower East Side Shows a Decline of $25,505,500 in Assessed Values," *New York Times*, October 16, 1932, sec. 10, 1.

CREATING THE LOWER EAST SIDE TENEMENT MUSEUM

1.   Ruth Abram, quoted in Robert E. Tomasson, "Orchard Street Tenement Project: A Chronicle of Immigrant Life," *New York Times*, December 31, 1990, 26.

2.   Tomasson, "Orchard Street."

3.   Lower East Side Tenement Museum, "Mission Statement," approved by the Board of Directors, October 1988.

4.   Judith Saltzman, "Preservation Philosophy," in *Lower East Side Tenement Museum Historic Structures Report* (New York: Lower East Side Tenement Museum, 2003).

5.   The five historic apartments represent the Moore family in 1869 just after the death of their daughter Agnes; the Gumpertz family in the 1878 when Natalie Gumpertz ran a dressmaking business in her apartment; the Rogarshevsky family in 1911 preparing for the Sabbath, the Levine family's tenement garment factory in 1897; and the Baldizzi family in 1935, on the day they were moving out of the apartment. The Confino family's apartment, depicting the year 1916, has been reconstructed in one of the former store spaces on the first floor.

6.   When the Rogarshevsky's apartment was first opened to the public, it told the story of Abraham Rogarshevsky's death from tuberculosis in 1920; in 2010, the theme was changed to focus on how families negotiate work and culture as they adapted to American conditions. New museum exhibitions have included the Irish Moore apartment opened in 2008; the backyard privy reconstruction in 2010; and the planning for the exhibition of the basement stores, interpreting the Schneider saloon and the Lustgarten's butcher shop was underway for a planned opening in 2012. Perkins Eastman was the architecture firm working with the museum on these projects. In 2011, the Tenement Museum initiated a series of tours that specifically address the building's fabric, introducing visitors to the many avenues of research and investigation undertaken by the museum's staff and consultants; see Lower East Side Tenement Museum, "Reading a Building Report" (2011).

INDEX

Note: Illustration entries appear in *italics*.